STEERING THE CRAFT

BOOKS BY URSULA K. LE GUIN

NOVELS
Always Coming Home
The Earthsea Books:
A Wizard of Earthsea
The Tombs of Atuan
The Farthest Shore
Tehanu
The Eye of the Heron
The Beginning Place
Malafrena
Very Far Away from Anywhere Else
The Word for World is Forest
The Dispossessed, An Ambiguous Utopia
The Lathe of Heaven
The Left Hand of Darkness
City of Illusion
Planet of Exile
Rocannon's World

STORIES
Unlocking the Air
Four Ways to Forgiveness
A Fisherman of the Inland Sea
Searoad
Buffalo Gals, and Other Animal Presences
The Compass Rose
Orsinian Tales
The Wind's Twelve Quarters

POETRY AND TRANSLATION
Lao Tzu: Tao Te Ching: A Book About
the Way and the Power of the Way
The Twins, the Dream/Las Gemelas, El
Sueño (with Diana Bellessi)
Going Out with Peacocks
Blue Moon Over Thurman Street (with
Roger Dorband)
Wild Oats and Fireweed
Hard Words
Wild Angels

CRITICISM
The Language of the Night
Dancing at the Edge of the World

FOR CHILDREN
The Catwings Books:
Catwings
Catwings Return
Wonderful Alexander and the Catwings
Jane on Her Own
Fish Soup
A Ride on the Red Mare's Back
Fire and Stone
A Visit from Dr. Katz
Solomon Leviathan
Cobbler's Rune
Leese Webster

SCREENPLAY IN BOOK FORMAT
King Dog

CHAPBOOKS
No Boats
In the Red Zone (with Henk Pander)
Tillai and Tylissos (with Theodora
Kroeber)
Walking in Cornwall
The Art of Bunditsu
A Winter Solstice Ritual (with Vonda N.
McIntyre)
Findings

EDITED
The Norton Book of Science Fiction
Edges (with Virginia Kidd)
Interfaces (with Virginia Kidd)
Nebula Award Stories 11

STEERING THE CRAFT

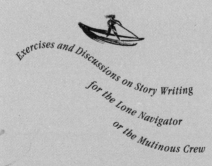

Exercises and Discussions on Story Writing for the Lone Navigator or the Mutinous Crew

URSULA K. LE GUIN

THE EIGHTH MOUNTAIN PRESS
PORTLAND • OREGON • 1998

Grateful acknowledgment is made for permission to reprint the following:

Excerpt from *The Fellowship of the Ring* by J.R.R. Tolkien, copyright 1954, 1965 by J.R.R. Tolkien and renewed 1982 by Christopher R. Tolkien, Michael H.R. Tolkien, John F.R. Tolkien and Priscilla M.A.R. Tolkien. Reprinted by permission of Houghton Mifflin Company.

Excerpt from *Jacob's Room* by Virginia Woolf, copyright 1922 by Harcourt Brace & Company and renewed 1950 by Leonard Woolf. Reprinted by permission of Harcourt Brace & Company.

Excerpts from *To the Lighthouse* by Virginia Woolf, copyright 1927 by Harcourt Brace & Company and renewed 1954 by Leonard Woolf. Reprinted by permission of Harcourt Brace & Company.

Excerpt from "Places Names" in *Dancing at the Edge of the World* by Ursula K. Le Guin, copyright 1981 by Ursula K. Le Guin. Reprinted by permission of Grove/Atlantic, Inc.

Quotations from Lynne Sharon Schwartz are from "Remembrance of Tense Past" in *Writers on Writing: A Breadloaf Anthology* selected and compiled by Jon Winokur (Middlebury College Press, 1991).

Cover design by Marcia Barrentine
Book design by Marcia Barrentine and Ruth Gundle

Manufactured in the United States of America
This book is printed on acid-free paper.
First edition 1998
10 9 8 7 6 5 4 3 2 1

LIBRARY OF CONGRESS CATALOGING-IN-PUBLICATION DATA
Le Guin, Ursula K., 1929–
    Steering the craft: exercises and discussions on story writing for the lone navigator or the mutinous crew / Ursula K. Le Guin. — 1st ed.
        p.   cm.
    ISBN 0-933377-46-0 (trade paper: acid-free paper). — ISBN 0-933377-47-9 (lib. bdg.: acid-free paper)
    1. Authorship—Problems, exercises, etc. 2. Creative writing—Problems, exercises, etc. 3. Narration (Rhetoric)—Problems, exercises, etc. I. Title.
PN212.L44 1998
808' .02—dc21   97-32587

THE EIGHTH MOUNTAIN PRESS
624 Southeast Twenty-ninth Avenue
Portland, OR 97214
phone: (503) 233-3936
fax: (503) 233-0774

CONTENTS

TABLE OF EXAMPLES

INTRODUCTION

"STEERING THE CRAFT" WAS THE NAME OF A WORKSHOP I GAVE AT FLIGHT of the Mind in 1996. The course description said we would work on punctuation, sentence length, verb person and tense, POV, voice, and other such technical aspects of narrative prose.

I offered the course because I'd been meeting a good many workshop writers who were afraid of semicolons and didn't know a Point of View from a Scenic Vista. It was supposed to be a workshop for people who needed to work on their navigational skills before they took the boat out across the Pacific.

What I got was fourteen experienced writers interested in their craft — people who had already thought about writing as a skill and wanted to think and talk about it some more. They were a joy to work with. Their input and feedback was invaluable to me, and if there's anything useful in what follows it's largely due to them.

What I've done here is to turn that workshop into a self-guided set of discussion topics and exercises for a writer, or a small group of writers, interested in the craft of narrative prose. I look forward very much to input and feedback from anybody who tries it. Please write to me at PO Box 10541, Portland, Oregon 97296-0541 and tell me what worked, what didn't work, and what I didn't think of that might work.

The Lone Navigator and the Mutinous Crew

Collaborative workshops and writers' peer groups◆ hadn't been invented when I was young. They're a wonderful invention.

They put the writer into a community of people all working at the same art, the kind of group musicians and painters and dancers have always had.

But I'd like to say here that one can attend many writing workshops and be a member of many peer groups and yet get no closer to finding one's own voice as a writer than one might do working alone in silence.

Groups offer, at their best, mutual encouragement, amicable competition, stimulating discussion, practice in criticism, and support in difficulty. These are great things, and if you're able to and want to join a group, do so! But if for any reason you can't, don't feel cheated or defeated. Ultimately you write alone. And ultimately you and you alone can judge your work. The judgment that a work is complete — *this is what I meant to do, and I stand by it* — can come only from the writer, and it can be made rightly only by a writer who's learned to read her own work. Group criticism is excellent training for self-criticism; but until quite recently no writer had that training, and yet they learned what they needed. They learned it by doing it.

If you and this book are alone together, I suggest that you try and work through it methodically, doing the exercises in order. When you've worked on an exercise till you're more or less satisfied with it, put it away and forbid yourself to look at it again for at least a week. That "cooling off" period is essential to revision. If there's one thing almost all writers agree on, it's that we can't trust our judgment on our own freshly written work. To see its faults and virtues we need to look at it after a real interval.

After a week or more, reread your piece with a friendly critical eye, with revision in mind. If I offer specific suggestions for criticism regarding the exercise, use them now. You might read the piece aloud to yourself, since speaking and hearing it may show up awkward bits and faults in the rhythm, and can help you make the dialogue natural and lively. In general, look for what's awkward, unclear, excessive, what breaks the pace, what doesn't work. Look for what *does* work, and admire it, and see if you can bring it out even better.

If you're working in a group, I recommend that in reading and critiquing the exercises you follow the workshop procedure outlined in Appendix I (The Peer Group Workshop). All my suggestions for group work are based on this procedure. I've used it for many years, in all the workshops I've led and peer groups I've belonged to. It works.

Each topical section introduces some matters "to think or talk about," which the lone navigator can mull over at leisure, and which, in a group, might help get a discussion going. And you'll bring to the group your own questions and topics, matters that have been on your mind or that arise from the discussions and exercises.

The Aim

The exercises are consciousness raisers: their aim is to clarify and intensify your awareness of certain elements of prose writing and certain techniques and modes of storytelling.

Once we're keenly and clearly aware of these elements of our craft, we can use and practice them until — the point of all the practice — we don't have to think about them consciously at all, because they have become skills.

A skill is something you know how to do.

Skill in writing frees you to write what you want to write. It may also show you what you want to write. Craft enables art.

There's luck in art. There's the gift. You can't earn that. You can't deserve it. But you can learn skill, you can earn it. You can learn to deserve your gift.

I'm not going to discuss writing as self-expression, as therapy, or as a spiritual adventure. It can be these things; but first of all — and in the end, too — it is an art, a craft, a making. To make something well is to give yourself to it, to seek wholeness, to follow spirit. To learn to make something well can take your whole life. It's worth it.

Storytelling

All the exercises are concerned with the basic elements of narrative: how a story is told, what moves and what clogs it, right down on the level of the elements of language.

The topics are:

- the sound of language
- punctuation, syntax, the narrative sentence and paragraph
- rhythm and repetition
- adjectives and adverbs
- tense and person of the verb
- voice and point of view
- implicit narration: imparting information
- crowding, leaping, focus, and control

As far as the exercises are concerned, it doesn't matter whether you write fiction or nonfiction, so long as it's narrative. A few problems are specific to fiction or to memoir, and I'll mention those I'm aware of, but in general, all storytellers work pretty much the same way, with the same box of tools.

Since narrative is what this is all about, my first suggestion is that you try to make each exercise not a static scene, but the account of an act or action. Write about something happening. Even if it's just a trip down a supermarket aisle or some thoughts going on inside a head, it should end up in a different place from where it started. That's what narrative does. It goes. It moves. Story is change.

The Exercises

Do make sure you understand the directions before you start writing the piece. Some of the directions are highly specific and may not be quite as simple as they look. Following them exactly will make the exercise useful.

Read the entire set of exercises under one number before you start to do any of them. This will help clarify what each one of them is about and how it differs from the others.

Do read all the discussion concerning an exercise before you do it.

Many of the exercise pieces you write will be very short, no more than a paragraph to a page or so. This is necessary if you're working in a group and reading your pieces aloud. Writing to a short, set length and not exceeding it is also an excellent discipline in itself. Of course your piece can grow longer, later, if it leads you into something interesting and you go on working on it.

My workshoppers told me it would be helpful if I suggested a subject or even a quite specific storyline or situation for each exercise, so I've done so. These aren't instructions or directions, but merely suggestions offered to those who don't want to sit around inventing a lot of stuff just in order to write an exercise. Unless the subject is part of the directions, as in Exercise Six, feel free to ignore these suggestions and write about anything you like.

Exercise pieces don't have to be highly finished; they don't have to be deathless literature. If they lead you on towards something bigger, that's grand. But to be successful as exercises, all they have to do is what the directions say to do.

If you're working in a peer group, you might choose to write some of the exercises during the meeting (in-class writing). After discussion of the exercise, each person writes it. Half an hour is the absolute time-limit. Silence: scribble scribble scribble. Then each one reads their piece aloud in turn, hot off the paper. The pressure often brings out excellent and surprising writing. In-class writing is particularly useful for people who aren't used to producing under pressure this way and think they can't do it (they can).

I mark the exercises I think work best for in-class writing with a ▲. The other exercises may need the kind of mulling over and rewriting that's best done in a room of one's own.

As for how to pace yourself, how long to allow to work and play with this book, that depends entirely on you. One Lone Navigator, testing it out, blitzed through it in a week — thus piling up an awful lot of exercise pieces to let cool and revise later. Taking a month or more might work best; you could start a new section every week or so. As for a Mutinous Crew, which meets only every fortnight or month, they might spend several months with the book.

In each section I give brief examples of various techniques, taken from notable writers, and discuss them a little. Do try reading them aloud, in the group or to yourself. (Don't be afraid of reading aloud alone! You'll only feel silly for a minute.)

The examples aren't meant to influence your style or approach when you write the exercise but only to show a variety of approaches to the technical problem in question. But if you want to try imitating one or another of them, do so. Students of composition and painting deliberately imitate great works of music and art as part of their training, but students of writing often seem afraid of imitation. Don't worry, it's not plagiarism to write a paragraph "in the style of" Austen or Dickens or Woolf. If you write it not as parody or pastiche but seriously, it can be a demanding and revealing exercise. I talk about this a little more on page 112.

Most of the examples quoted in the book are taken from older works of fiction, partly because permission to quote from contemporary works is often expensive or unavailable, but mostly because I love and am familiar with these older books. The idea of being familiar with a "classic" is foreign to many people, or even scary. All too often I meet writers who've read hardly anything written before their own lifetimes, and whose understanding of what a writer can do with the English language is therefore sadly limited. I hope some of these examples, which I chose because I love them, may lead such readers past the forbidding labels, "classic" or "Victorian" or whatever, to the living reality of the great novels.

After these quoted examples I may suggest some authors or books (often more recent ones) that demonstrate masterful handling of one or many of the topics of the exercises. An attentive reading of some of these books, with a consciousness of technique in mind, would be useful as well as enjoyable.

The examples and the suggestions for further reading make good subjects for group discussion or for private study. What is this writer doing, how is she doing it, why is she doing it, do I like it? Finding other examples, bringing them to the group, discussing them, could be profitable to everybody in the crew. And the lone navigator may find guides, companions, dear friends among the writers who have also sailed these seas and found their way through the reefs and shoals.

I use as little technical language as possible, but every trade has its jargon. So there's a small glossary of technical or fancy terms for those who, up to now, have managed to avoid them. The first time I use such words I mark them with a ♦.

She slipped swift as a silvery fish
through the slapping gurgle of sea-waves.

ONE

THE SOUND
OF YOUR WRITING

HE SOUND OF THE LANGUAGE IS WHERE IT ALL BEGINS AND WHAT it all comes back to. The basic elements of language are physical: the noise words make and the rhythm of their relationships. This is just as true of written prose as it is of poetry, though the sound-effects of prose are usually subtle and always irregular.

Most children enjoy the sound of language for its own sake. They wallow in repetitions and luscious word-sounds and the crunch and slither of onomatopoeia;◆ they fall in love with musical or impressive words and use them in all the wrong places. Some writers keep this childish love for the sounds of language. For them language is not a way to deliver a message, but, as McLuhan said, *is* the message. Others "outgrow" their oral/aural sense of language as they learn to read in silence. That's a loss. I think an awareness of what your own writing sounds like is an essential skill for a writer. Fortunately it's one quite easy to cultivate, to relearn, reawaken.

A good reader has a mind's ear. Though we read most of our narratives in silence, a keen inner ear does hear them. Dull, choppy, droning, jerky, feeble: these are all faults in the sound of prose, though we may not know we hear them as we read. Lively, well-paced, flowing, strong, beautiful: these are all qualities of the sound of prose, and we rejoice in them as we read. And so good writers train their mind's ear to listen to their own prose — to hear as they write.

Now the chief duty of a narrative sentence is to lead to the next sentence — to keep the story going. I'll come back to this point, which is important, in Exercise Three. But pace and movement depend above all on rhythm, and you have to hear your writing to feel its rhythm. So at this point, to encourage listening, I want to encourage free play — play with the rhythms and sounds of the sentences you write.

We think of poetry as getting to be gorgeous and prose as having to be plain; but consider what's going on in the following examples. (Read them aloud! Read them aloud loudly!)

EXAMPLE

1

Gertrude Stein: "Susie Asado"

Sweet sweet sweet sweet sweet tea.
  Susie Asado.
Sweet sweet sweet sweet sweet tea.
  Susie Asado.
Susie Asado which is a told tray sure.
  A lean on the shoe this means slips slips hers.
  When the ancient light grey is clean it is yellow, it is
a silver seller.
  This is a please this is a please there are the saids
to jelly. These are the wets these say the sets to leave
a crown to Incy.
  Incy is short for incubus.
  A pot. A pot is a beginning of a rare bit of trees.

Trees tremble, the old vats are in bobbles, bobbles
which shade and shove and render clean, render clean
must.
       Drink pups.
  Drink pups drink pups lease a sash hold, see it
shine and a bobolink has pins. It shows a nail.
      What is a nail. A nail is unison.
      Sweet sweet sweet sweet sweet tea.

This little piece by Gertrude Stein has no narrative impulse at all and verges on the lyric poem, but I wanted some Stein here, and this is such a neat, sweet bit.

EXAMPLE
2

Rudyard Kipling: "How the Whale Got His Throat" from *Just So Stories*

"Noble and generous Cetacean, have you ever tasted Man?"

"No," said the Whale. "What is it like?"

"Nice," said the small 'Stute Fish. "Nice but nubbly."

"Then fetch me some," said the Whale, and he made the sea froth up with his tail.

"One at a time is enough," said the 'Stute Fish. "If you swim to latitude Fifty North, longitude Forty West (that is magic), you will find, sitting *on* a raft, *in* the middle of the sea, with nothing on but a pair of blue canvas breeches, a pair of suspenders (you must *not* forget the suspenders, Best Beloved), and a jack-knife, one shipwrecked Mariner, who, it is only fair to tell you, is a man of infinite-resource-and-sagacity."

So the Whale swam and swam to latitude Fifty North, longitude Forty West, as fast as he could swim, and *on* a raft, *in* the middle of the sea, *with* nothing to wear except a pair of blue canvas breeches, a pair of suspenders (you must particularly remember the suspenders, Best Beloved), *and* a jack-knife, he found one single, solitary shipwrecked Mariner, trailing his toes in the water. (He had his mummy's leave to paddle, or else he would never have done it, because he was a man of infinite-resource-and-sagacity.)

Then the Whale opened his mouth back and back and back till it nearly touched his tail, and he swallowed the shipwrecked Mariner, and the raft he was sitting on, and his blue canvas breeches, and the suspenders (which you *must* not forget), *and* the jack-knife — He swallowed them all down into his warm, dark, inside cupboards, and then he smacked his lips — so, and turned round three times on his tail.

The *Just So Stories* are a masterpiece of exuberant vocabulary, musical and dramatic phrasing, and humor. Kipling has given countless children a lifelong sense of the pure beauty of language.

EXAMPLE

3

Mark Twain: from "The Celebrated Jumping Frog of Calaveras County"

"Well, thish-yer Smiley had rat-tarriers, and chicken cocks, and tomcats and all them kind of things, till you couldn't rest, and you couldn't fetch nothing for him to bet on but he'd match you. He ketched a frog one day, and took him home, and said he cal'lated to educate him; and so he never done nothing for three months but set in his back yard and learn that frog to jump. And you bet you he *did* learn him, too. He'd give him a little punch behind, and the next minute you'd see that frog whirling in the air like a doughnut — see him turn one summerset, or maybe a couple, if he got a good start, and come down flat-footed and all right, like a cat. He got him up so in the matter of ketching flies, and kep' him in practice so constant, that he'd nail a fly every time as fur as he could see him. Smiley said all a frog wanted was education, and he could do 'most anything — and I believe him. Why, I've seen him set Dan'l Webster down here on this floor — Dan'l Webster was the name of the frog — and sing out, 'Flies, Dan'l, flies!' and quicker'n you could wink he'd spring straight up and snake a fly off'n the counter there, and flop down on the floor ag'in as solid as a gob of mud, and fall to scratching the side of his head with his hind foot as indifferent as if he hadn't no idea he'd been doin' any more'n any frog might do. You never see a frog so modest and straightfor'ard as he was, for all he was so gifted. And when it come to fair and square jumping on a dead level, he could get over more ground at one straddle than any animal of his breed you ever see. Jumping on a dead level was his strong suit, you understand; and when it come to that, Smiley would ante up money on him as long as he had a red. Smiley was monstrous proud of his frog, and well he might be, for fellers that had traveled and been everywheres all said he laid over any frog that ever *they* see."

This passage from Mark Twain's early story, "The Celebrated Jumping Frog of Calaveras County," is totally aural/oral, its beauty lying in its irresistible dialectical cadences. There are lots of ways to be gorgeous.

Ursula K. Le Guin: from "Places Names" in
Dancing at the Edge of the World

After breakfast at Lums, the Entire Lums Family
  Thanks You,
comes the Child Evangelism Camp, and Harmony
  Grove,
and Pruntytown, 1798, Founded by John Prunty.
And we come over Laurel Mountain and from the top see
  all the misty ridges
and coming down we're into the Eastern Seaboard smog,
  that yellow bile
that you see from airplanes, the yellow breath of our
  god.
Nite Crawlers 75 cents a dozen,
beside the Cheat River, a misty mirror for the hills.
Into Maryland at Backbone Mountain
and then right back into West Virginia, a state all
  backbone,
loyal to the union.
       Mineral County.
       Mount Storm.
       The Knobley Farm, 1766, on knobbly hills
       Ridgeville village on the hogback ridge
       Hampshire County, 1754, we keep going back
       The Stone House
       Little Cacapon River
       Paw Paw, on Short Mountain.
         Where ye bin, honey?
                 I bin to Paw Paw, maw.
       WELCOME TO VIRGINIA!
                Jesus is coming ready or not.
And it's left one mile to Mecca, and right one mile to
  Gore.
We'd better go straight on.
So we went on to Georgia.

This bit from my travel piece "Places Names" is very free prose. It uses line breaks to help the reader to make pauses in the flow of words, many of them road signs or names of towns, which I wrote while riding shotgun on a drive down the East Coast. Its gorgeousness is totally localised and its narrative quality consists simply in that movement forward.

A Note on Names

Names are very interesting sounds; and names are often under the fiction writer's control — names of characters: Uriah Heep...Jane Eyre...Beloved.... The sounds themselves and the echo-allusions hidden in them are intensely evocative. Names of places, too. Faulkner knew what he was doing with Yoknapatawpha County. To me one of the most deeply evocative invented (or to be exact, borrowed) names is Tolkien's plain and simple name for the world of his fantasy: Middle Earth.

You might think or talk about character's names and place-names you like in fiction, and what it is you like about them, what it is about the sound of them that makes them meaningful even if you can't "translate" the meaning.

FURTHER READING

Some books that I relish particularly for the splendor of their language are Zora Neale Hurston's *Their Eyes Were Watching God*, Alice Walker's *The Color Purple*, Judy Grahn's *Mundane's World*. Fantasy is a form of narrative essentially dependent on its language; several classics of English prose are fantasies, such as *Alice in Wonderland*. The conscious beauty of language of such fantasists as Lord Dunsany or E.R. Eddison may be as intoxicating to read as it is dangerous to imitate.

This first exercise is a warm-up, a playtime piece, to get you listening to the sound of your writing.

BEING GORGEOUS

Write a paragraph to a page (150–300 words) of narrative that's meant to be read aloud. Use onomatopoeia, alliteration,◆ repetition, rhythmic effects, made-up words or names, dialect — any kind of sound-effect you like — *but NOT rhyme or meter.*◆

This is a read-aloud piece — performance prose. Loosen up, it won't ever be printed! Write it for children, if that's the only way you can give yourself permission to do it. Whatever you do, have fun, cut loose, play around with word sounds and rhythms. Make what happens happen in the sounds of the words, the rhythms of the sentences. Say it aloud, as you write and/or after you write.

I say don't use rhyme because if you do, or if you use any regular meter, you're writing verse; and this is a prose exercise.

I really hesitate to suggest any "plot" for this one, but if you simply can't get an idea for it, you might try doing the climax of a ghost story. Or invent an island and describe it.

Performing and listening to these pieces in a group can be a lot of fun. Not much critiquing◆ will be called for, probably. The best response to a performance piece is applause, with appreciation of the particularly effective bits. If you're working alone, do read your piece out loud, with vigor. Doing so will almost certainly lead you to improve it here and there, play some more with it, make the sound of it still stronger and livelier.

To think or talk about afterward: Did concentrating on the sound of the writing release or enable anything unusual or surprising, a voice you haven't often used? Did you enjoy doing the exercise, or was it a strain? Can you say why?

It's a highly repeatable exercise, by the way, and can serve as a warm-up more than once. If you do it again, you might try for a different set of sound-effects, creating a different mood entirely. Look at the view out the window or the mess on the desk, or remember something that happened yesterday or something weird that somebody said, and make a gorgeous sentence or two or three out of it. It might get you into the swing of writing.

Damn the semicolons cried the captain full speed ahead

Two

PUNCTUATION

HE POET CAROLYN KIZER SAID TO ME RECENTLY, "POETS ARE IN-terested mostly in death and commas," and I agreed. Now I add: Prose writers are interested mostly in life and commas.

If you aren't interested in punctuation, or are afraid of it, you're missing out on a whole kit of the most essential, beautiful, elegant tools a writer has to work with.

There's not much I can do about it here. What you need to do is get hold of *The Elements of Style*, by Strunk and White, and more or less memorize it. It is in some respects a little old-fashioned, but not elitist. It is intellectually and aesthetically honest and noble. It is charming, funny, and implacable. The only rules you are ever going to get from me are all in Strunk and White. You will find just about the same rules, with lots of very funny examples and illustrations, in Karen Gordon's *The Well-Tempered Sentence: A Punctuation Handbook for the Innocent, the Eager, and the Doomed*.

Opinion Piece on Grammatical Correctness

Now that we've talked about rules of punctuation, which lead straight into rules of grammar♦ and usage, and before we go any further, I want to talk about grammatical correctness.

Almost all of us were scared stiff by the teacher who scolded us in second grade — "Billy, it's wrong to say 'It's me.' Say, 'It is I.'" Most of us are still afraid of the columnist who sneers at us in the newspaper — "Illiterate boors who say '*Hopefully* we can be there!'" Such people take a very moralistic stance on grammar.

But then, so did Socrates. He said, "The misuse of language induces evil in the soul." I've had that sentence pinned up over my desk for a long time.

Lying is the misuse of language. We know that. We need to remember that it works the other way round too. Even with the best intentions, language misused, language used stupidly, carelessly, brutally, language used wrongly, breeds lies, half-truths, confusion.

In that sense you can say that grammar is morality. And it is in that sense that I say a writer's first duty is to use language well.

But Socrates wasn't talking about "correctness." That's not a moral issue, but a social and political one. "Correct grammar," "correct usage," are used as tests or shibboleths to form an in-group of those who speak and write English "correctly" and an out-group of those who don't. And guess which group has the power?

How we talk is important to us all, and we're all shamed when told in public that we don't talk correctly. Shame can paralyse our minds. Many common misusages are actually overcorrections. People scolded for saying "It's me" may start saying "Between you and I," because they have an uneasy feeling that *me* is incorrect, a bad word, to be avoided.

I detest the self-righteous tones of those who sneer at other people's speech, and I distrust their motives. But I have to walk a razor's edge here in this book, because the fact is that "incorrect" usage, in written prose, unless part of a conscious, consistent dialect voice, is disastrous. It can invalidate a whole piece.

How can a reader trust a writer who seems to be ignorant of the medium she works in?

Our standards for writing are higher and more formal than for speaking. They have to be, because when we read, we don't have the speaker's voice and expression and intonation to make half-finished sentences and misused words clear. We have only the words. *They* must be clear. And, to be clear to as many readers as possible, they have to follow the generally agreed-upon rules, the shared rules, of grammar and usage.

Whatever the writer does has to be within the frame of *knowing* those shared expectations. Only if you know the rule can you break it.

Here's an example: I often use the possessive pronoun "their" in the singular: On page 13 I wrote, "Each one reads their piece aloud in turn." This is "incorrect," say the grammarians, because *each one, each person* is a singular noun, and *their* is a plural pronoun. But Shakespeare used *their* with words such as *everybody, anybody, a person;* and so we all do when we're talking. ("It's enough to drive anyone out of their senses," said George Bernard Shaw.) The grammarians only started telling us it was "incorrect" along in the sixteenth or seventeenth century, when they also declared that "he" includes both sexes. As in: "If a person needs an abortion, he should be required to tell his parents."

Do I have to say that my use of "their" is politically motivated, and, if you like, politically correct? It's a deliberate response to the socially and politically significant banning of our genderless pronoun by language-legislators.

But it isn't grammatically incorrect. It's just pushing it a little. I know what I'm doing.

And that's the important thing for any writer: to know what we're doing with our language.

For all of us, this involves avoiding ungrammatical, overcorrected, or colloquial♦ usages that stick out painfully in written prose. They're not morally wrong and their social significance is irrelevant — but they can make a written sentence *sound* all wrong. And that's what matters.

To think or talk about before doing the exercise: What problems do you have with punctuation? What do you feel uncertain about? What rules are you impatient with?

If you have a group to talk with, talk about these matters. It's reassuring to know that everybody worries about semicolons. Every writer, that is. People who don't worry at least a little about semicolons aren't likely to be writers.

In the long term, it's worth looking up the things that worry you. See if some real thinking about them, maybe some practice using the examples in Strunk and White or Gordon as models to imitate, makes you begin to feel easy with these usages.

If punctuation is something you've generally avoided thinking about, you might sit down all by yourself and go through a few paragraphs of prose narratives that you like and admire, and just study the punctuation in them. What's the author doing, why did she break that sentence that way, why did she want a pause there, how much of the rhythm of the prose is actually established by the punctuation, how's it done?

▲E X E R C I S E T W O

I AM GARCÍA MÁRQUEZ

Write a paragraph to a page (150–350 words) of narrative *with no punctuation* (and no paragraphs or other breaking devices).

Suggested Subject: A group of people engaged in a hurried or hectic or confused activity, such as a revolution, or the first few minutes of a one-day sale.

To think or talk about in critiquing the exercise: How well does the unbroken flow of words fit the subject? To what extent does the unpunctuated flow actually shape the narrative?

For a group: The likelihood is that, read aloud by the author, the piece wasn't too hard to follow. Is it comprehensible to another person reading it silently?

To think about after writing it: What writing it felt like; how it differed from writing with the usual signs and guides and breaks; whether it led you to write differently from the way you usually write, or gave you a different approach to something you've tried to write. Was the process valuable? Is the result readable?

A week later: It may be interesting, now, to go through your piece and punctuate it. The nonpunctuated passage had to find a way to make itself clear without punctuation. To punctuate it may involve rewriting it. Which version do you think works better?

❖ ❖ ❖

I will now tell the Panda Story to illustrate the importance of the presence or the absence of the comma. This panda walked into a tea shop and ordered a salad and ate it. Then it pulled out a pistol, shot the man at the next table dead, and walked out. Everyone rushed after it, shouting, "Stop! Stop! Why did you do that?"

"Because I'm a panda," said the panda. "That's what pandas do. If you don't believe me, look in the dictionary."

So they looked in the dictionary and sure enough they found *Panda: Raccoon-like animal of Asia. Eats shoots and leaves.*

The wind died. The sail fell slack.

The boat slowed, halted.

We were becalmed.

THREE

SENTENCE LENGTH AND COMPLEX SYNTAX*

As I said before, when we were being gorgeous: The chief duty of a narrative sentence is to lead to the next sentence.

Beyond this basic, invisible job, the narrative sentence can do an infinite number of beautiful, surprising, powerful, audible, visible things (see *all* the examples). But the basic function of the narrative sentence is to keep the story going and keep the reader going with it.

Its rhythm is part of the rhythm of the whole piece; all its qualities are part of the quality and tone of the whole piece. As a narrative sentence, it isn't serving the story well if its rhythm is so unexpected, or its beauty so striking, or its similes* or meta- phors* so dazzling, that it stops the reader, even to say Ooh, Ah! Poetry can do that. Poetry can be visibly, immediately dazzling. In poetry a line, a few words, can make the reader's breath catch and her eyes fill with tears. But for the most part, prose sets its proper beauty and power deeper, hiding it in the work as a whole. In a story it's the *scene* — the setting/characters/action/

interaction/dialogue/feelings — that makes us hold our breath, and cry…and turn the page to find out what happens next. And so, until the scene ends, each sentence should lead to the next sentence.

Rhythm is what keeps the song going, the horse galloping, the story moving. Sentence length has a lot to do with the rhythm of prose. So an important aspect of the narrative sentence is — prosaically — its length.

Teachers trying to get school kids to write clearly, and journalists with their weird rules of writing, have filled a lot of heads with the notion that the only good sentence is a short sentence.

This is true for convicted criminals.

Very short sentences, isolated or in a series, are terrifically effective in the right place. Prose consisting entirely of short, syntactically simple sentences is monotonous, choppy, a blunt instrument. If short-sentence prose goes on very long, whatever its content, the thump-thump beat gives it a false simplicity that soon just sounds dumb. See Spot. See Jane. See Spot bite Jane.

Narrative prose consisting largely of long, complex sentences, full of embedded clauses♦ and all the rest of the syntactical armature,♦ is fairly rare these days. Some people have never read any and so are anxious about reading it, let alone writing it. Very long sentences have to be carefully and knowledgeably managed, solidly constructed; their connections must be clear, so that they flow, carrying the reader along easily.

It's a myth that short-sentence prose is "more like the way we speak." A writer can build a sentence in a more deliberate way than a speaker can, because a writer can revise. But a lot of people who are nervous about constructing a long sentence in writing actually speak in long, well-articulated♦ sentences. People following a complex thought aloud often do so by using a wealth of clauses♦ and qualifiers. Dictation, indeed, is notoriously wordy.♦ When Henry James began dictating his novels to a secretary, his tendency to qualify and parenthesize and embed clause within clause got out of hand, clogging the narrative flow and making his prose totter on the edge of self-parody. Listening with a careful ear to one's prose isn't the same thing as falling in love with the sound of one's voice.

To avoid long sentences and the marvelously supple connections of a complex syntax is to deprive your prose of an essential quality. Connectedness is what keeps a narrative going.

As Strunk and White say, variety in sentence length is what's needed. All short will sound stupid. All long will sound stuffy.

In revision you can consciously check for variety, and if you've fallen into a thumping of all short sentences or a wambling of all long ones, change them to achieve a varied rhythm and pace.

What the sentence says and does is essential in determining its length:

"Kate fires the gun." — A short sentence.

"Kate perceives that her husband's not paying any real attention to what she's saying to him, but also observes that she doesn't much care if he's paying attention or not, and that this lack of feeling may be a sinister symptom of something she doesn't want to think about just now." — This kind of subject may well require a complicated sentence that can work itself out at some length.

EXAMPLE

5

Jane Austen: from *Mansfield Park*

As a general reflection on Fanny, Sir Thomas thought nothing could be more unjust, though he had been so lately expressing the same sentiments himself, and he tried to turn the conversation; tried repeatedly before he could succeed; for Mrs. Norris had not discernment enough to perceive, either now, or at any other time, to what degree he thought well of his niece, or how very far he was from wishing to have his own children's merits set off by the depreciation of hers. She was talking *at* Fanny, and resenting this private walk half through the dinner.

It was over, however, at last; and the evening set in with more composure to Fanny, and more cheerfulness of spirits than she could have hoped for after so stormy a morning; but she trusted, in the first place, that she had done right, that her judgment had not misled her; for the purity of her intentions she could answer; and she was willing to hope, secondly, that her uncle's displeasure was abating, and would abate farther as he considered the matter with more impartiality, and felt, as a good man must feel, how wretched, and how unpardonable, how hopeless and how wicked it was, to marry without affection.

When the meeting with which she was threatened for the morrow was past, she could not but flatter herself that the subject would be finally concluded, and Mr. Crawford once gone from Mansfield, that every thing would soon be as if no such subject had existed. She would not, could not believe, that Mr. Crawford's affection for her could distress him long; his mind was not of that sort. London would soon bring its cure. In London he would soon learn to wonder at his infatuation, and be thankful for the right reason in her, which had saved him from its evil consequences.

Jane Austen's prose is still near enough the balanced style of the eighteenth century that it may sound stately or overcomposed to a modern ear; but read it aloud and I think you'll hear how vivid and versatile it is and feel its easy strength. (The dialogue in several recent film versions of Austen novels was taken unchanged from the books.) The syntax is complex but clear. Many of the connections that lengthen the sentences are semicolons, so that most of these sentences would have been equally "correct" if Austen had used periods instead of semicolons. Why didn't she? — The second paragraph is all one sentence. If you read it aloud you'll hear how the length of the sentence gives weight to the last clause of it. Yet it isn't heavy, because it's broken into rhythmic repetitions: "How wretched, and how unpardonable, how hopeless and how wicked it was...."

Harriet Beecher Stowe: from *Uncle Tom's Cabin*

Over such a road as this our senator went stumbling
along, making moral reflections as continuously as
under the circumstances could be expected, — the
carriage proceeding along much as follows, — bump!
bump! bump! slush! down in the mud! — the senator,
woman and child, reversing their positions so suddenly as to come, without any very accurate adjust-
ment, against the windows of the down-hill side.
Carriage sticks fast, while Cudjoe on the outside is
heard making a great muster among the horses. After
various ineffectual pullings and twitchings, just as the
senator is losing all patience, the carriage suddenly
rights itself with a bounce, — two front wheels go
down into another abyss, and senator, woman, and
child, all tumble promiscuously on to the front seat, —
senator's hat is jammed over his eyes and nose quite
unceremoniously, and he considers himself fairly
extinguished; — child cries, and Cudjoe on the outside
delivers animated addresses to the horses, who are
kicking, and floundering, and straining under repeated
cracks of the whip. Carriage springs up, with another
bounce, — down go the hind wheels, — senator,
woman, and child, fly over on to the back seat, his
elbows encountering her bonnet, and both her feet
being jammed into his hat, which flies off in the
concussion. After a few moments the "slough" is
passed, and the horses stop, panting; — the senator
finds his hat, the woman straightens her bonnet and
hushes her child, and they brace themselves for what
is yet to come.

This funny bit from *Uncle Tom's Cabin* consists of a couple of
long sentences, loosely connected, in onomatopoeic imitation of

what she's writing about — an interminable, jolting, chaotic journey. Stowe is not what's called a "great stylist," but she is an absolutely first-rate storyteller. Her prose does what she wants it to and carries us right along with it.

EXAMPLE

7

Mark Twain: from *The Adventures of Huckleberry Finn*

...then we set down on the sandy bottom where the water was about knee deep, and watched the daylight come. Not a sound, anywheres — perfectly still — just like the whole world was asleep, only sometimes the bull-frogs a-cluttering, maybe. The first thing to see, looking away over the water, was a kind of dull line — that was the woods on t'other side — you couldn't make nothing else out; then a pale place in the sky; then more paleness, spreading around; then the river softened up, away off, and warn't black any more, but gray; you could see little dark spots drifting along, ever so far away — trading scows, and such things; and long black streaks — rafts; sometimes you could hear a sweep screaking; or jumbled-up voices, it was so still, and sounds come so far; and by-and-by you could see a streak on the water which you know by the look of the streak that there's a snag there in a swift current which breaks on it and makes that streak look that way; and you see the mist curl up off of the water, and the east reddens up, and the river, and you make out a log cabin in the edge of the woods, away on the bank on t'other side of the river, being a wood-yard, likely, and piled by them cheats so you can throw a dog through it anywheres; then the nice breeze springs up, and comes fanning you from over there, so cool and fresh, and sweet to smell, on account of the woods and the flowers; but sometimes

not that way, because they've left dead fish laying
around, gars, and such, and they do get pretty rank;
and next you've got the full day, and everything
smiling in the sun, and the song-birds just going it!

The beautiful passage from *Huckleberry Finn* could exemplify
a lot of things, but let's use it as an example of a very long sentence (consisting of short or fairly short subsentences strung together by semicolons) which catches the rhythm and even the
voice quality of a person talking aloud — quietly. You can't orate
this passage, you can't belt it out. It has its own voice — Huck's
voice, which is understated and totally unassuming. It's calm,
gentle, singsong. It flows, as quiet as the river and as sure as the
coming of day. The words are mostly short and simple. There's
a bit of syntax that the grammarians would call "incorrect,"
which snags up and flows on just exactly like the snag and the
water that it describes. There's some dead fish, and then the sun
rises, and it's one of the great sunrises in all literature.

EXAMPLE

8

Virginia Woolf: from "Time Passes"
in *To the Lighthouse*

Then indeed peace had come. Messages of peace
breathed from the sea to the shore. Never to break its
sleep any more, to lull it rather more deeply to rest,
and whatever the dreamers dreamt holily, dreamt
wisely, to confirm — what else was it murmuring —
as Lily Briscoe laid her head on the pillow in the clean
still room and heard the sea. Through the open
window the voice of the beauty of the world came
murmuring, too softly to hear exactly what it said —
but what mattered if the meaning were plain? entreat-
ing the sleepers (the house was full again; Mrs.
Beckwith was staying there, also Mr. Carmichael), if

they would not actually come down to the beach itself at least to lift the blind and look out. They would see then night flowing down in purple; his head crowned; his sceptre jewelled; and how in his eyes a child might look. And if they still faltered (Lily was tired out with travelling and slept almost at once; but Mr. Carmichael read a book by candlelight), if they still said no, that it was vapour, this splendour of his, and the dew had more power than he, and they preferred sleeping; gently then without complaint, or argument, the voice would sing its song. Gently the waves would break (Lily heard them in her sleep); tenderly the light fell (it seemed to come through her eyelids). And it all looked, Mr. Carmichael thought, shutting his book, falling asleep, much as it used to look.

Indeed, the voice might resume, as the curtains of dark wrapped themselves over the house, over Mrs. Beckwith, Mr. Carmichael, and Lily Briscoe so that they lay with several folds of blackness on their eyes, why not accept this, be content with this, acquiesce and resign? The sigh of all the seas breaking in measure round the isles soothed them; the night wrapped them; nothing broke their sleep, until, the birds beginning and the dawn weaving their thin voices in to its whiteness, a cart grinding, a dog somewhere barking, the sun lifted the curtains, broke the veil on their eyes, and Lily Briscoe stirring in her sleep. She clutched at her blankets as a faller clutches at the turf on the edge of a cliff. Her eyes opened wide. Here she was again, she thought, sitting bolt upright in bed. Awake.

In this passage notice the variety of sentence length, the complexity of the syntax, including the use of parentheses, and the rhythm thus obtained, which flows and breaks, pauses, flows again — and then, in a one-word sentence, stops.

There is going to be more Virginia Woolf in this book than any other author. I find her thought and work wonderful in itself and useful to anyone thinking about how to write. The rhythm of Woolf's prose is to my ear the subtlest and strongest in English fiction. She said this about it, in a letter to a writer friend: "Style is a very simple matter; it is all rhythm. Once you get that, you can't use the wrong words. But on the other hand here am I sitting after half the morning, crammed with ideas, and visions, and so on, and can't dislodge them, for lack of the right rhythm. Now this is very profound, what rhythm is, and goes far deeper than words. A sight, an emotion, creates this wave in the mind, long before it makes words to fit it...."

I've never read anything that says more about the mystery at the very center of what a writer does.

FURTHER READING

Marcel Proust's *Remembrance of Things Past* as translated by C.K. Scott Moncrieff is a famous repository of sentences that go on and on and on. Less pretentiously literary, Patrick O'Brian's series of sea novels (it begins with *Master and Commander*) contains sentences so marvelously clear, vivid, and fluent that one can't believe they go on as long as they do. Gabriel García Márquez experiments with nonstop sentences and with omission of paragraphing in several of his novels, which is why I named the exercise after him. I can't find any examples of very good writing notable for its short sentences. Maybe this is significant; maybe it's just my taste.

▲ E X E R C I S E   T H R E E

SHORT AND LONG

Part One: Write a paragraph of narrative, 100–150 words, in sentences of seven or fewer words. No sentence fragments!◆ Each must have a subject and a verb.

Part Two: Write a half-page to a page of narrative, up to 350 words, which is all one sentence.

Suggested Subjects: For Part One, some kind of tense, intense action — like a thief entering a room where someone's sleeping....

For Part Two: A very long sentence is suited to powerful, gathering emotion, and to sweeping a lot of characters in together. You might try some family memory, fictional or real, such as a key moment at a dinner table or at a hospital bed.

Note: Short sentences don't have to consist of short words; long sentences don't have to consist of long ones. If you find this happening in your prose, you might try, just out of contrariness or curiosity, to counteract the tendency.

In critiquing, it may be interesting to discuss how well the short or long sentences fit the story being told. Do the short sentences read naturally? How is the long sentence constructed — carefully articulated pieces, or one torrent? Is the syntax of the long sentence clear and assured, so that the reader doesn't get lost and have to go back and start over? Does it read easily?

To think or talk about after writing: If either part of the exercise forced you into writing in a way you'd never ordinarily choose to write, consider whether this was enjoyable, useful, maddening, enlightening, etc., and why.

It might be entertaining to take a page or so of narrative prose that you like and study its sentences (and paragraphing). Simply count words per sentence and sentences per paragraph, list them, and look at the amount of variation. If you can't stand that kind of thing, at least read a favorite narrative passage aloud, listening specifically for the variety and interplay of sentence lengths, and the kind of rhythm the sentences establish.

Later on: You may want to return to this exercise, which has a lot of possibilities.

OPTIONAL REVISITS TO EXERCISE THREE

Part One: If you wrote the exercise the first time in an authorial or formal voice, try the same or a different subject in a colloquial, even a dialect voice — perhaps a character talking to another character.

If you did it colloquially to start with, back off a little and try a more detached, authorial mode.

Part Two: If your long sentence was syntactically simple, connected mainly with ands or semicolons, try one with some fancy clauses and stuff — show Henry James how.

If you already did that, try a more "torrential" mode, using ands, dashes, etc. — let it pour out!

Both Parts: If you told two different stories in the two different sentence lengths, you might try telling the same story in both, and see what happens to the story.

The PARAGRAPH should come here, because, like the sentence, it's a key element in the ordering and articulation of the narrative as a whole. However, an exercise in paragraphing would have to be pages long before it could be useful. And it's hard to discuss paragraphing in the abstract. The main thing is, it's important: something to think about, something to consider when revising. It matters where you put those little indents. They show connections and separations in the flow; they are architecturally essential, part of the structure and the long rhythmic pattern of the work.

The following is rather tendentious, so I set it as:

 *An Opinion Piece on Paragraphing*

I have found in several how-to-write books statements such as, "Your novel should begin with a one-sentence paragraph," "No paragraph in a story should contain more than four sentences," and so on. Rubbish! Such "rules" originated in periodicals printed in columns — newspapers, pulp magazines, *The New Yorker* — which really do have to break the tight grey density of the print with frequent indents, large initial caps, and line breaks. If you publish in such periodicals, expect to let the editors add breaks and paragraph indents. But you don't have to do it to your own prose. "Rules" about keeping sentences and paragraphs short are mechanical spin-offs from journalism and a highly artificial school of "action" writing. If you obey them, you'll probably sound like second-class Hemingway. If that's what you want, that's how to achieve it. To me it's only worse than sounding like first-class Hemingway. But then, it takes all sorts.

The sudden wind brought rain,

a cold rain on a cold wind.

FOUR

REPETITION

GAIN I AM INCLINED TO FAULT JOURNALISTS AND SCHOOLTEACHERS, however well meaning, for declaring it a sin to say the same word twice, driving people to the thesaurus in desperate searches for farfetched substitutes.

Repetition can indeed be awkward when a word is emphasized for no reason: "He was studying in his study. The book he was studying was Plato." This kind of thing comes of not listening to one's writing (and from the long thinking-pauses that occur while writing, so that you've forgotten the last sentence when you start a new one.) Everybody does it. It's easy to fix in revision by finding a synonym or a different phrasing: "He was in his study, reading Plato and making notes," or whatever.

But to make a rule "never use the same word twice in one paragraph," or to state flatly that repetition is to be avoided, is to throw away one of the most valuable tools of narrative prose. Repetition of words, of phrases, of images; repetition of things said; near-repetition of events; echoes, reflections, variations:

from the grandmother telling a folktale to the most sophisticated novelist, all narrators use these devices, and the skillful use of them is a very great part of the power of prose.

Prose can't rhyme and chime and repeat a beat as poetry can, or if it does it had better be subtler about it than the first half of this sentence. The rhythms of prose — and repetition is the central means of achieving rhythm — are usually hidden or obscure, not obvious. They may be long and large, involving the whole shape of a story, the whole course of events in a novel: so large they're hard to see, like the shape of the mountains when you're driving on a mountain road. But the mountains are there.

EXAMPLE

9

"The Thunder Badger" from Marsden, *Northern Paiute Language of Oregon*, a word-by-word translation, slightly adapted by U.K.L.

He, the Thunder, when he is angry that the earth has dried up, that he has no moist earth, when he wants to make the earth moist, because the water has dried up:

He, the Thunder, the Rain Chief, lives on the surface of the clouds. He has frost; he, the Thunder Sorcerer, appears like a badger; the Rain Sorcerer, he, the Thunder. After he digs, he lifts up his head to the sky, then the clouds come; then the rain comes; then there is cursing of earth; the thunder comes; the lightning comes; evil is spoken.

He, the real badger, only he, white stripes on his nose, here on his back. He it is, only the badger, this kind. He, the Thunder Sorcerer, that does not like dried-up earth when he is digging, when he is scratching this way. Then raising his head to the sky, he makes the rain; then the clouds come.

"The Thunder Badger" is sacred or ritual narrative, an oral form that predates the distinction of prose from poetry. All such narration is completely fearless about repetition, using it openly and often, both to shape the story and to give the words their due majesty and power. This Paiute story isn't heavy-duty sacred, just ordinarily sacred. It should be told, like most stories, only in the winter. I apologize for retelling it out of season, but it really must be read aloud.

Folktales often repeat themselves exuberantly, both in the language and in the structure: consider "The Three Bears," with its cascade of European triads. (Things in Europe happen in threes, things in Native American folktales often happen in fours.) Stories written to read aloud to children use a lot of repetition. Kipling's *Just So Stories* (see Example Two) are a splendid example of repetition used as incantation, as a structural device, and to make you and the child laugh.

Repetition is often funny. The first time David Copperfield hears Mr. Micawber say, "Something is certain to turn up," it doesn't mean much to David or to us, but by the time we've heard Mr. Micawber, forever hopeful in his incompetence, say the same or nearly the same words throughout the long book, it is very funny. The reader waits for it, as for the inevitable and delightful repetition of a musical phrase in Haydn. But also, every time Mr. Micawber says it, it means more. It gathers weight. The darkness underneath the funniness grows always a little darker.

Structural repetition is the similarity of the events in a story, happenings that echo one another. It's hard to talk about or give an example of in a brief space, as it involves the whole of a story or novel. If you're familiar with *Jane Eyre*, you might reread the first chapter of it, and think about the rest of it as you do. (If you haven't read *Jane Eyre*, do; then you can think about it, possibly for the rest of your life.) The first chapter contains a good deal of "foreshadowing," the introduction of images and themes that will be repeated throughout the book. For example: we meet Jane as a shy, silent, self-respecting child, the outsider in an unloving household, who takes refuge in books, pictures, and nature. The older boy who bullies and abuses her goes too far at last, and she turns on him and fights back. Nobody takes her part, and she's locked in an upstairs room that she's been told is haunted. —

Well, grown-up Jane is going to be the shy outsider in another household, where she'll stand up against Mr. Rochester's bullying, finally be forced to rebel, and find herself utterly alone. And there's an upstairs room at Thornfield which is, indeed, "haunted." The first chapters of many great novels bring in an amazing amount of material that will be, in one way and another, with variations, repeated throughout.

The similarity of this incremental repetition of word, phrase, image, and event in prose to recapitulation and development in musical structure is real and deep.

E X E R C I S E F O U R : P A R T S **1 & 2**

AGAIN AND AGAIN AND AGAIN

I can't suggest "plots" for these; the nature of the exercise doesn't allow it.

▲ *Part One:* Verbal Repetition
Write a paragraph of narrative (150 words) that includes at least three repetitions of a noun, verb, or adjective (a noticeable word, not an invisible one like "was," "said," "did").
This exercise can easily be done in a group as in-class writing. (If you read it aloud, don't tell people what the repeated word is; do they hear it?)

Part Two: Syntactic Repetition
Write a paragraph to a page of narrative (200–400 words) in which you deliberately repeat the *syntactical construction*, or the *exact rhythm*, of a phrase or sentence (or more than one) several times.

"Repeat the syntactical construction": if this isn't clear, let me give an example of what I'd like you to do:

With her hands in her pockets, she walked to the door and faced the stranger. His eyes on her face, he stood there a moment and said nothing.

Do you see how the second sentence exactly repeats the construction of the first one, even though all the words are different?

You can do the same thing with the rhythm:

We always went to the mountain in summer. But I never knew what had happened to Bonny.

The "But" is a swing-word connecting two sentences that are exactly alike in their rhythm. If you don't hear the sameness, say them aloud, chant them, and you will.

Deliberate, exact repetition of this kind is not a technique to use in story-writing; it's an exercise in awareness. It's highly technical, rather difficult, and can be quite satisfying. If you carry it on very long, of course, the prose gets monotonous. The fun is to keep that from happening as long as you can. This is best done by yourself, not in class; it calls for constant checking back and forth and revision while writing, and you don't want to hurry it.

EXERCISE FOUR: PART 3

Part Three: Structural Repetition

Write a short narrative (350–1000 words) in which something is said or done, and then something is said or done that echoes or repeats it, perhaps in a different context, or by different people, or on a different scale.

This can be a complete story, if you like, or a fragment of narrative.

Any two parts of this exercise, or all three, may be combined into one.

In critiquing, you might concentrate on the effectiveness of the repetitions and their obviousness or subtlety.

To think or talk about after writing: Were you comfortable at first with the idea of deliberately repeating words and constructions and events? Did you get more comfortable with it doing it? Did the exercise bring out any particular feeling-tone or subject matter or style in your work, and can you say what it was?

I'm not sure how free the nonfiction writer is to use structural repetition. To force unlike events into a repetitive pattern certainly would be cheating. But to seek for likeness, for pattern, in the events of a life surely is one of the memoirist's goals? All this is worth discussing and thinking about.

Look for examples of structural repetition in fiction and nonfiction (and if you have a group, share and recommend them). An awareness of how repetition and echoing contribute to the structure and the pattern of narrative can add greatly to your appreciation of a good story.

We completed the voyage without succumbing to the temptation of opening the box of candy.

FIVE

ADJECTIVE
AND ADVERB

DJECTIVES AND ADVERBS ARE RICH AND GOOD AND FATTENING. THE main thing is not to overindulge.

When the quality that the adverb indicates can be put in the verb itself (they ran quickly = they raced) or the quality the adjective indicates can be put in the noun itself (a growling voice = a growl), the prose will be cleaner, more intense, more vivid.

In Chapter Five of *The Elements of Style,* Strunk and White talk about the abuse of qualifiers. The qualifiers I myself have to look out for are "kind of," "sort of," and "just" — and always, always "very." You might just look at your own writing to see if you have some very favorite qualifiers that you kind of use just a little too often.

Some adjectives and adverbs have become meaningless through literary overuse. "Great" seldom carries the weight it ought to carry. "Suddenly" seldom means anything at all; it's a mere transition device, a noise — "He was walking down the street. Suddenly he saw her." "Somehow" is a weasel word; it

means the author didn't want to bother thinking out the story —
"Somehow she just knew...." "Somehow they made it to the asteroid...." When I teach science fiction and fantasy writing I ban the word. Nothing can happen "somehow."

Ornate, fancy adjectives are out of fashion. Nobody much is likely to say that anything is sesquipedalian, these days. But some conscious prose stylists use adjectives as poets do: the adjective's relation to the noun is unexpected, farfetched, forcing the reader to stop and make the connection. This mannerism can be effective, but in narration it's risky. Do you want to stop the flow? Is it worth it?

I would recommend to all storytellers a watchful attitude and a thoughtful, careful choice of adjectives and adverbs, because the bakery shop of English is rich beyond belief, and narrative prose, particularly if it's going a long distance, needs more muscle than fat.

EXERCISE FIVE

CHASTITY

Write a paragraph to a page (200–350 words) of descriptive narrative prose without adjectives or adverbs. No dialogue.

The point is to give a vivid description of a scene or an action, using only verbs, nouns, pronouns, and articles. Adverbs of time (then, next, later, etc.) may be necessary, but be sparing. Be chaste.

If you're using this book in a group, I recommend that you do this exercise at home, because it may take a while.

If you're currently working on a longer piece, you might want to try writing the next paragraph or page of it as this exercise.

The first time you do the exercise, write something new. After that you might want to try "chastening" a passage you've already written. It can be interesting.

Critiquing: With this exercise, it's above all the doing of it that matters, and your own judgment on the result. Would the piece be improved by the addition of an adjective or adverb here and there, or is it satisfactory without? Critiquing may address these questions. Readers may also catch a stray adjective you missed. In the group or working alone, notice the devices and usages you were forced into by the requirements of the exercise. It may have affected particularly your choice of verbs and your use of simile and metaphor.

I invented the Chastity Exercise for my own use when I was a very Lone Navigator of fourteen or fifteen. I couldn't give up chocolate milkshakes, but I could do without adverbs for a page or two. It's the only exercise I've suggested in (I think) every workshop I've taught. It seems to be useful to us all.

The old woman dreamed of the past as she navigated the seas of time.

SIX

SUBJECT PRONOUN AND VERB

_T_HIS SECTION IS ABOUT THE PERSON◆ OF THE VERB AND THE TENSE◆ of the verb. The exercise involves both, since a verb without subject or tense is in the infinitive, which won't get a story far (though it makes a great beginning to one soliloquy we know).

First, however, I want to say something about the passive voice.

Opinion Piece on the Passive Voice

Passive constructions, such as those used in the sentence presently being read by you, are far too frequently employed in the writing of academic papers and business correspondence, and those whose efforts have been to see this usage reduced are to be commended.

But I find that many people who yatter on about banning the passive voice don't even know what it is. They have confused it with the verb to be (which grammarians so sweetly call "the copulative").

"There are three great oaks on the road to Doomthorpe." This is not a passive construction. I think it has a fancy name, but I'll just call it the There-is construction. Many verbs are more exact and colorful than the verb *to be*, but you tell me how else Hamlet should have started that soliloquy. It's a good idea not to use the There-is construction excessively; for instance, the sentence above might be stronger as: "Three great oaks stand on the road to Doomthorpe." But there is nothing inherently wrong with There-is, and there are good reasons for using it in the right place.

And none of this has anything to do with the passive voice.

"A hole was dug in the ground by gnomes." Passive.

"Gnomes dug a hole in the ground." Active.

"It was proposed that the motion be tabled." Two passives.

"Ms. Brown proposed that the committee table the motion." Two actives.

People often use the passive voice because it's indirect, polite, unaggressive, and admirably suited to making thoughts seem as if nobody had personally thought them and deeds seem as if nobody had done them, so that nobody need take responsibility. Thus the passive is beloved of bureaucrats and timid academics, and generally shunned by writers who do want to take responsibility. The cowardly writer says, "It is believed that being is constituted by ratiocination." The brave writer says, "I think, therefore I am."

If your style has been corrupted by long exposure to academese or "business English," you may need to worry about the passive. Make sure it hasn't seeded itself where it doesn't belong. If it has, root it out as needed. Where it does belong, I think we ought to use it freely. It is one of the lovely versatilities of the verb.

Person of the Verb

The persons available to narrative are first singular (I) and third singular (she, he), with limited use of first and third plural (we, they). The second person (you) is available to poets. (A few stories and one or two novels have been written, painfully, in the second person.)

Almost all preliterate, sacred, and literary prose narrative before the sixteenth century is in the third person. First-person writing begins, I think, with medieval diaries and saints' confessions, with Montaigne and Erasmus, and early travel narratives. In early fiction, evidently a justification was wanted for presenting a character other than the author as "I." A letter writer naturally writes "I": hence the epistolary novel. Since the eighteenth century, fiction written in the first person has been so common that we think nothing about it, but in fact it's an odd, sophisticated imaginative process both for the writer and for the reader.

Exercise Six may involve using the "limited third person." This is a term having to do with Point of View, which we'll be working on in the next set. If you're not familiar with the term, all you need to know about it at this point is that in "limited third" you're writing from inside your story character. You can tell *only* what that single character perceives, feels, knows, remembers, guesses.

Let's say you're writing the story from Della's point of view. You can say, "Della looked up into Rodney's adoring face," but you can't say, "Della raised her incredibly beautiful violet eyes to Rodney's adoring face." Why not? Because although Della may be aware she's incredibly beautiful and has violet eyes, that's not what *Della* sees when she looks up. That's what *Rodney* sees. And Della is the person whose mind you're in. Only Della's perceptions are perceptible. Rodney's aren't. And if Della really is thinking about the color of her own eyes, instead of how adorably adoring Rodney looks, you have to explain why: "She raised her eyes, knowing the effect their violet beauty would have on him."

If this still seems mysterious, consider that the limited third person is very like the first person in some ways; and you know that when you write as "I" you can tell only what "I" see and know. — "I raised my incredibly beautiful violet eyes to Rodney's adoring face." I'm sure you see why you wouldn't write *that*.

(*Private aside:* Why do heroines have to have either violet or green eyes? Is it a requirement? It's tiresome. And unjust. Men in fiction never get to have violet eyes, and if they have green ones they're almost always the villain.)

FURTHER READING

First-person narration is so common both in fiction and memoir that I hesitate to single out any book or books from the hundreds of excellent examples of it. But I do urge you to read anything written by Grace Paley. Her stories avoid all the pitfalls of first-person narration — posing, egotism, self-consciousness, monotony. They seem like artless little things — just some woman telling you about something. They are masterpieces of art.

Again, so many modern novels are told in the limited third person that recommendation becomes arbitrary. But I recommend that, for a while at least, you *notice* what person(s) the book you're reading is written in, and whether and when and how it changes person.

Tense of the Verb

Narrative tense is a complex subject. It's something prose writers need to think about, to be conscious of, so they can choose the tense appropriate to the effect they want.

My discussion of it is another opinion piece, a long one. I hope it sets off discussions and arguments, disagreements and agreements, and so serves to clarify your, and my, thinking. I should state here that the following discussion relates only to the so-called "standard" English dialect. The conjugation of the verb and distinction of the tenses in black English deserves a discussion of its own, which I would read with interest and profit.

Opinion Piece on Narrative Tense

The Paradox

A sentence in the present tense: *I know where I'm going*.

A sentence in the past tense: *I knew where I was going*.

To discuss the use of tense, we have to realize that in fictional and nonfictional narrative, the "past tense" is not past and the "present tense" is not present. Both are entirely fictive. The story, whether or not it's based on a real event, exists only on the page. The only real present time is the reader's.

In order to avoid these paradoxes, some critics call the two principal narrative tenses "remote" and "actual," but these terms are useless except as propaganda. "Actual" is untrue, and who wants to have their story labelled "remote"?

When we're talking about the use of the tenses in narrative prose, I'd like to call the past tense the "inclusive narrative tense," and the present the "focussed narrative tense." If anybody else finds these terms useful, please use them.

Some General Observations

My impression is that in talking aloud, most of us use the past tense to tell a story of real events, shifting easily over into the present tense, often at an exciting moment. Like this: "I was walking down the street yesterday, I wasn't thinking about anything except maybe I wanted to go into the coffee shop and get a cappuccino, and suddenly I see this man who looks exactly like Abraham Lincoln! And he's wearing a propeller beanie!"

When written history, memoir, and fiction embed a present-tense scene in past-tense narration it's called "the historical present."

Abstract discourse — such as this essay — is always in the present tense. Generalities aren't time-bound. Philosophers, physicists, and God all speak in the present tense. (Seeking equal authority with the physical sciences, anthropologists used to write, "The Ussu worship forest spirits," even when the last three Ussu were Mormon converts working for the lumber mill. This is an example of how ethical issues can get attached to something that seems as utterly value-neutral as a verb tense. Many anthropologists have by now decided not to confuse their science with eternal verity, and to describe what's past as past.)

Screenplays are written in the present indicative tense, but with an imperative meaning — screenplays are directions concerning what *has to happen* on screen. "Dick grins at Jane, fires. Blood spatters lens. CU: Spot falls dead." These aren't descriptions. They're instructions, telling the actors, cameraman, ketchup person, dog, etc., what to do.

The only genuine narrative present tense I know is *concurrent reporting,* which is usually oral: "Oh, my God, it's catching fire —" or "He's crossing the fifty-yard line, he's in the clear now!" When journalists write, "Sources close to the President report that he is considering a veto," this too may be a genuine present tense. Concurrent reporting used to be rare; the media have made it common. The apparent (mostly illusory) immediacy of media reporting undoubtedly encourages use of the present tense in narration.

I think the mere name, "present tense," leads some writers to assume that present-tense narration implies immediacy — a story-time close to the reader's present. Therefore they assume that use of the past tense implies a remoter time. This is naive. It doesn't work that way. I've read effective stories in which recent events were told in the past tense and the present tense was used for what happened a long time ago. The tenses have so little connotation of actual presentness or pastness that, in that respect, they're interchangeable. But they do have different implications regarding continuity.

Continuity and Immediacy

"Once upon a time there was a king who had a daughter as beautiful as the day...."

That time, once-upon-a-time, story-time, contains all times.

The reason I call the past tense the "inclusive narrative tense" is that it posits a time that had a past and will have a future. It includes other times.

Using the past tense, the writer can move around in time easily by using the past perfect, the future perfect, and the various moods and forms of the verb (which we use all the time without thinking about it, but which, if their names are unfamiliar, you'll find in Appendix II). By giving easy access to times before and after the period of the narrative, this tense includes a vast historical and narrative context. It implies continuity.

"The king walks up and down the throne room scolding his daughter...."

I call the present tense the "focussed narrative tense" because it sacrifices the larger time-field to achieve keen, close focus. In the present tense, narration is linear, leading to the next moment, excluding global temporal reference. Writing narrative in the present tense, use of the simple or compound past tenses becomes awkward and use of the future highly artificial. The present tense implies discontinuity.

This focussed narrative tense, which used to be rare in fiction and nonexistent in memoir, is now extremely common. I should admit that its trendiness prejudices me against it. I have used it, and appreciated its use; I understand why its very discontinuity makes it valuable for a writer in a disconnected, incoherent world.

But its supposed immediacy, its "presentness," is as fictive as the pastness of fiction written in the past tense, and far more artificial. Present-tense narrative uses the same temporal vocabulary as the past tense. We don't write, "She slaps the Velcro fasteners on her Adidas, now gets up and stretches." We write, "She slaps the Velcro fasteners on her Adidas, then gets up and stretches." Only if we were concurrently reporting a real event, like a TV sports commentator, could we use *now*. We use *then* because this isn't the present, isn't actual. Fact or fiction, it's a story. Whether we're conscious of it or not, we know the difference between actuality and story, and we use the appropriate vocabulary.

This paradoxicality may attract writers to the present tense. It is a technique, rather than a voice. Forced to move with a staccato awkwardness, it's more visible than the past tense. A bright beam tightly focussed, it affords the writer and reader the detachment of visible artifice. It distances. It cuts out. It keeps the story cool. If the writer's engine is liable to overheat, focussed narrative may be a wise choice.

But it's unwise to use it without considering its limitations and its implications. In an excellent piece on the subject, the novelist Lynne Sharon Schwartz says that when she asked writers why they used the present tense they all said it gave a greater feeling of "immediacy," and when I've asked the question I've received the same answer. It sounds plausible, but I mistrust it. A narrow focus isn't more immediate: it merely leaves out more. By avoiding temporal context and historical trajectory, present-tense narrative simplifies the world, suggesting, as Schwartz says, that nothing "is terribly complex and that understanding, such as it is, can be achieved by naming objects or accumulating data," and that "all we can ever understand is what can be understood from a glimpse." This avoidance of complexity leads away from inwardness, either of the characters' or of the author's mind. So it may gain vividness, clarity, a linear simplicity, at the cost of a great deal else — including real, felt immediacy.

Neither Schwartz nor I argue with the maxim "Show, don't tell," if it means that it's better to narrate through examples not generalities, to be vivid not vague. But we both question the maxim when it's extended to mean: List actions and objects, but don't interpret, lest you be seen as judgmental; don't show emotion, lest you be seen as unsophisticated; keep your voice impersonal, lest you risk a genuinely immediate relationship to your reader.

By suppressing the shared past that connects writer and reader, and by its tendency to relate actions externally, the present tense flattens the affect♦ of the writer's voice. From this flatness derives the curious sameness of present-tense narrative. It all sounds rather alike. Perhaps this sameness explains its current popularity. It's bland, predictable, risk-free. All too often, it's McProse.

The wealth and complexity of our verb forms is part of the color of the language. Using only one tense is like having a whole set of oil paints and using only pink.

I suspect some people write in the present tense because they're afraid of the other tenses. (She had had some trouble with the past perfect tense in an earlier life. In her next life, she will not be going to have any trouble with the future perfect. But she would have liked never to have had any trouble at all.)

If you're hesitant about some of the past tenses, practice using them. You do know them. All that stuff is in your head, and has been ever since you learned to say "I went" instead of "I goed." But if you don't read narratives written before 1970, and if you've always written in the present tense, some of these patterns may not have been activated for a long time. To regain free use of them is to increase your range of options as a storyteller. There are times the present tense is the right one, and there are times the past tense is the right one. Let yourself be able to make the choice.

On Two-Timing

There's one thing about tense usage that I could almost state as a rule, but I won't, because good and careful writers will always blow any such rule into bits. So I state it as a high probability.

It is highly probable that if you go back and forth between past and present tense, if you switch the tense of your narrative frequently and without some kind of signal (a line break, a dingbat,◆ a new chapter) your reader will get all mixed up as to what happened before what and what's happening after which and when we are, or were, at the moment.

Such confusions often occur even when writers switch tenses deliberately. When they do it without knowing they're doing it — when they're simply unconscious of what tense they're writing in, and go flipping back and forth from present to past to present — it is highly probable that the reader will end up seasick, sullen, and indifferent to what happened, let alone when.

The following short passage is from a modern novel. Not wanting to embarrass the author, I change names and actions to make the scene unrecognizable, but I reproduce the syntax and the verb numbers and tenses exactly.

They both come in wanting coffee. We hear Janice
playing the TV in the other room. I noticed Tom had a

black eye that I didn't see last night. "Did you go out?"
I said.

Tom sits down with the paper and says nothing.

Alex says, "We both went out."

I drank two cups of coffee before I said anything.

Is it possible to read this without noticing that it changes tense three times in six lines? (To be exact, it changes tense five times, since the simple past "I didn't see" refers to a time previous to the present; but it occurs in a past-tense sentence, where a previous time would normally be indicated by the past perfect "I hadn't seen.") Is it possible to say that anything is gained by this incoherence, which continues throughout the book? I can't believe that the author was even aware of it. But that's an awful thing to say.

A tense switch in written narrative isn't a minor thing. It's a big deal, like changing viewpoint characters. It can't be done mindlessly. It can be done invisibly, but only if you're good at it.

So it's worthwhile to think, before changing tenses in mid-story, whether you have any reason for doing so. And when you do so, it's worthwhile to make sure you carry your readers effortlessly with you, and don't maroon them, like the hapless crew of the *Enterprise*, in a Temporal Anomaly that they can get out of only by using Warp Speed Ten.

E X E R C I S E   S I X

THE OLD WOMAN

This should run to a page or so; keep it short and not too ambitious, because you're going to have to write the same story at least twice.

The subject is this: An old woman is

washing the dishes, or gardening, or editing a Ph.D. dissertation in mathematics, or...whatever you like, as she thinks about an event that happened in her youth.

You're going to write this sketch by *intercutting* between the two times. "Now" is the kitchen, the garden, the desk, whatever, and "then" is what happened when she was young. Your narration will *move back and forth* between "now" and "then." There should be *at least two* of these moves or time-jumps.

Version One:

Choose a PERSON:
  a) first person (I)
  b) third person (her name/she)

Choose a TENSE:
  a) all in past tense
  b) all in present tense
  c) "now" in present tense, "then" in past tense
  d) "now" in past tense, "then" in present tense

Write the story. Label it — *Person (a), Tenses (c)* — or whichever you chose.

Version Two: Now write the same story *in the other person* and a *different choice of tenses.* (Label it.)

Don't strain to keep the wording of the two versions identical, and please don't just go through it on a computer changing the pronoun and the verb endings. Write it over. Changing the person and tense will almost certainly bring about some changes in the wording, the telling; and these changes are interesting.

Within one version, the verb tense may shift, but the person of the verb can't. Stick with either "I" or "she" in Version One. Then use the other person in Version Two.

Additional Option: If you want to go on and play with all four tense options, do.

Another Additional Option: After you have done the exercise as directed, if you want to change the person of the verb within one version (using one person in "now," the other person in "then"), try it.

Critiquing: If you wrote more than two versions, pick only two for your group to read — four or five versions of the same little story is too much to ask of them. It may be useful to discuss the ease or awkwardness of the time-shifts; how well suited the tenses chosen are to the material; which pronoun works best for this story; which choice or combination of tenses works best for this story; whether there's much difference between the two versions and if there is, what is it; and, if anybody tried the last option, whether this device works at all and what its effect is.

To think or talk about after writing it: If you're in a group, discussion of the subject of the exercise may rise out of the critiquing process. People are likely to have quite different reactions to the same piece.

If you're pondering these things alone, it can be useful to read narrative prose, for a while, with a particular consciousness of what persons and tenses of the verb are used, why the author may have used them, how well they're used, what effect they give, whether and how often and why the narrative tense is changed.

I saw he was lost in his memories, like a boat

that drifts on its own reflection.

SEVEN

POINT OF VIEW
AND VOICE

OINT OF VIEW, POV FOR SHORT AND WHEN SCRIBBLED IN MARGINS of manuscripts, is the technical term for describing *who is telling the story and what their relation to the story is.*

This person, if a character in the story, is called the *viewpoint character.* (The only other person it can be is the author.)

Voice is a word critics often use in discussing narrative. It's always metaphorical, since what's written is voiceless. Often it signifies the authenticity of the writing (writing in your own voice; catching the true voice of a kind of person; and so on). I'm using it naively and pragmatically to mean *the voice or voices that tell the story,* the narrating voice. For our purposes in this book, at this point, I'll treat voice and point of view as so intimately involved and interdependent as to be the same thing.

The Principal Points of View

What follows is my attempt to define and describe the five principal narrative points of view. Each description is followed by an example: a paragraph told in that POV, from a nonexistent story called "Princess Sefrid." It's the same scene each time, the same people, the same events. Only the viewpoint changes.

A Note on the "Reliable Narrator"

In autobiography and memoir, in nonfiction narrative of any kind, the "I" (whether the writer uses it or not) is the author. In these forms, the reader has a right, I think, to expect the author/narrator to be reliable — to try to tell us as honestly as possible what happened. Reading nonfiction, we assume that the author is not inventing, but relating, and won't change facts to make the story neater — at least, not blatantly.

In fiction, the "I" narrator (or the third-person narrator) is *not* the author. Most first- and third-person narrators in serious fiction used to be trustworthy, just like memoirists. But "unreliable narrators" are now fairly common in fiction, narrators who — deliberately or innocently — misrepresent the facts.

Fictional narrators who suppress facts, or who make mistakes in relating or interpreting the events, are almost always telling us something about themselves (and perhaps about us.) The author lets us see or guess what "really" happened, and using this as a touchstone, we readers are led to understand how other people see the world, and why they (and we?) see it that way.

A familiar example of a semireliable narrator is Huck Finn. Huck misinterprets a good deal of what he sees. For instance, he never understands that Jim is the only adult in his world who treats him with love and honor; he never really understands that he loves and honors Jim. The fact that he *can't* understand it tells us an appalling truth about the world he and Jim — and we — live in.

Princess Sefrid, as you will see by comparing her relation with those of other viewpoint characters, is entirely reliable.

First Person

In first-person narration, the viewpoint character is "I." "I" tells the story and is centrally involved in it. Only what "I" knows, feels, perceives, thinks, guesses, hopes, remembers, etc., can be told. The reader can infer what other people feel and who they are only from what "I" sees, hears, and says of them.

Princess Sefrid: First Person Narration

I felt so strange and lonesome entering the room crowded with strangers that I wanted to turn around and run, but Rassa was right behind me, and I had to go ahead. People spoke to me, asked Rassa my name. In my confusion I couldn't tell one face from another or understand what people were saying to me, and answered them almost at random. Only for a moment I caught the glance of a person in the crowd, a woman looking directly at me, and there was a kindness in her eyes that made me long to go to her. She looked like somebody I could talk to.

Limited Third Person

The viewpoint character is "he" or "she." "He" or "she" tells the story and is centrally involved in it. Only what the viewpoint character knows, feels, perceives, thinks, guesses, hopes, remembers, etc., can be told. The reader can infer what other people feel and are only from what the viewpoint character observes of their behavior. This limitation to the perceptions of one person may be consistent throughout a whole book, or the narrative may shift from one viewpoint character to another. Such shifts are usually signalled in some way, and usually don't happen at very short intervals.

Tactically, limited third is identical to first person. It has exactly the same essential limitation: that nothing can be seen, known, or told except what the narrator sees, knows, and tells. That limitation concentrates the voice and gives apparent authenticity.

It seems that you could change the narration from first to limited third person by merely instructing the computer to switch the pronoun, then correct verb endings throughout, and *voilà*. But it isn't that simple. First person is a different voice from limited third. The reader's relationship to that voice is different — because the author's relationship to it is different. Being "I" is not the same as being "he" or "she." In the long run, it takes a quite different imaginative energy, both for the writer and for the reader.

There is no guarantee, by the way, that the limited third person narrator is reliable.

"Stream-of-consciousness"♦ is a particularly inward form of limited third person.

Princess Sefrid: Limited Third Person

Sefrid felt isolated, conspicuous, as she entered the room crowded with strangers. She would have turned around and run back to her room, but Rassa was right behind her, and she had to go ahead. People spoke to her. They asked Rassa her name. In her confusion she could not tell one face from another or understand what people said to her. She answered them at random. Only once, for a moment, a woman looked directly at her through the crowd, a keen, kind gaze that made Sefrid long to cross the room and talk to her.

Involved Author ("Omniscient Author")

The story is not told from within any single character. There may be numerous viewpoint characters, and the narrative voice may change at any time from one to another character within the story, or to a view, perception, analysis, or prediction that only the author could make. (For example: the description of what a person who is quite alone looks like; or the description of a landscape or a room at a moment when there's nobody there to see it.) The writer may tell us what anyone is thinking and feeling, interpret behavior for us, and even make judgments on characters.

This is the familiar voice of the storyteller, who knows what's going on in all the different places the characters are at the same time, and what's going on inside the characters, and what has happened, and what has to happen.

All myths and legends and folktales, all young children's stories, almost all fiction until about 1915, and a vast amount of fiction since then, use this voice.

I don't like the common term "omniscient author," because I hear a judgmental sneer in it. I think "authorial narration" is the most neutral term, and "involved author" the most exact.

Limited third person is the predominant modern fictional voice — partly in reaction to the Victorian fondness for involved-author narration, and the many possible abuses of it.

Involved author is the most openly, obviously manipulative of the points of view. But the voice of the narrator who knows the whole story, tells it because it is important, and is profoundly involved with *all* the characters, cannot be dismissed as old-fashioned or uncool. It's not only the oldest and the most widely used storytelling voice, it's also the most versatile, flexible, and complex of the points of view — and probably, at this point, the most difficult for the writer.

Princess Sefrid: Involved Author ("Omniscient Author")

The Tufarian girl entered the room hesitantly, her arms close to her sides, her shoulders hunched; she looked both frightened and indifferent, like a captured wild animal. The big Hemmian ushered her in with a proprietary air and introduced her complacently as "Princess Sefrid," or "the Princess of Tufar." People pressed close to meet her or simply to stare at her. She endured them, seldom raising her head, replying to their inanities briefly, in a barely audible voice. Even in the pressing, chattering crowd she created a space around herself, a place to be lonely in. No one touched her. They were not aware that they avoided her, but she was. Out of that solitude she looked up to meet a gaze that was not curious, but open, intense, compassionate — a face that said to her, through the sea of strangeness, "I am your friend."

Detached Author ("Fly on the Wall," "Camera Eye," "Objective Narrator")

There is no viewpoint character. The narrator is not one of the characters, and can say of the characters only what a neutral observer (an intelligent fly on the wall) might infer of them from behavior and speech. The author never enters a character's mind. People and places may be exactly described, but values and judgments can be implied only indirectly. A popular voice around 1900 and in "minimalist" and "brand-name" fiction, it is the most covertly manipulative of the points of view.

It's excellent practice for writers who expect codependent readers. When we're new at writing we may expect our readers to respond just as we respond to what we're writing about — to cry because we're crying. But this is a childish, not a writerly, relation to the reader. If you can move a reader while using this cool voice, you've got something really moving going on.

Princess Sefrid: Detached Author ("Fly on the Wall," "Camera Eye," "Objective Narrator")

The princess from Tufar entered the room followed closely by the big man from Hemm. She walked with long steps, her arms close to her sides and her shoulders hunched. Her hair was thick and frizzy. She stood still while the Hemmian introduced her, calling her Princess Sefrid of Tufar. Her eyes did not meet the eyes of any of the people who crowded around her, staring at her and asking her questions. None of them tried to touch her. She replied briefly to everything said to her. She and an older woman near the tables of food exchanged a brief glance.

The narrator is one of the characters, but not the principal character — present, but not a major actor in the events. The difference from first-person narration is that the story is not about the narrator. It's a story the narrator witnessed and wants to tell us. Both fiction and nonfiction use this voice.

Princess Sefrid: Observer-Narrator in First Person

> She wore Tufarian clothing, the heavy red robes I had not seen for so long; her hair stood out like a storm cloud around the dark, narrow face. Crowded forward by her owner, the Hemmian slavemaster called Rassa, she looked small, hunched, defensive, but she preserved around herself a space that was all her own. She was a captive, an exile, yet I saw in her young face the pride and kindness I had loved in her people, and I longed to speak with her.

Observer-Narrator, Using the Third Person

This point of view is limited to fiction. The tactic is much the same as the last one. The viewpoint character is a limited third-person narrator who witnesses the events.

As unreliability is a complex and subtle way of showing the *narrator's* character, and the observer-narrator isn't the protagonist, the reader is usually safe in assuming this viewpoint character is reliable, or at least perfectly transparent, both in first and third person.

Princess Sefrid: Observer-Narrator in Third Person

> She wore Tufarian clothing, the heavy red robes Anna had not seen for fifteen years. Crowded forward by her

owner, the Hemmian slavemaster called Rassa, the princess looked small, hunched, defensive, but she preserved around herself a space that was all her own. She was a captive, an exile, yet Anna saw in her young face the pride and kindness she had loved in the Tufarians, and longed to speak with her.

FURTHER READING

Look at a bunch of stories in an anthology or pull down a bunch of novels from your shelf (from as wide a span of time as possible) and identify the viewpoint character(s) and the point(s) of view of the narration. Notice if they change, and if so, how often.

Considerations on Changing Point of View

I'm going into all this detail because the narrative problem I meet most often in workshop stories (and often in published work) is in handling POV: inconsistency and frequent changes of POV.

It's a problem even in nonfiction, when the author starts telling the reader what Aunt Jane was thinking and why Uncle Fred swallowed the grommet. A memoirist doesn't have the right to do this without clearly indicating that Aunt Jane's thoughts and Uncle Fred's motives aren't known facts, but the author's guesswork, opinion, or interpretation. Memoirists can't be omniscient, even for a moment.

In fiction, inconsistent POV is a very frequent problem. Unless handled with awareness and skill, frequent POV shifts jerk the reader around, bouncing in and out of incompatible identifications, confusing emotion, garbling the story.

Any shift from one of the five POVs outlined above to another is a dangerous one. It's a major change of voice to go from first to third person, or from involved author to observer-narrator. The shift will affect the whole tone and structure of your narrative.

Shifts within limited third person — from one character's mind to another's — call for equal awareness and care. A writer must be aware of, have a reason for, and be in control of all shifts of viewpoint character.

I feel like writing the last two paragraphs all over again, but that would be rude. Could I ask you to read them over again?

The POV exercises are intended to make you temporarily super-conscious, and forever conscious, of what POV you're using and when and how you shift it.

Limited third is, at present, the person most fiction writers are most used to using. First person is, of course, the voice memoirists mostly use. I think it's a good idea for all of us to try all the other possibilities.

Fiction writers are used to writing in other people's voices, being other selves. But memoirists aren't. To use limited third person in factual narrative is to trespass, pretending you know what another real person thought and felt. But there's no problem with pretending you know what somebody you *invented* thinks and feels. So I recommend that, just for the exercise, memoirists invent a story, make up characters, in the shameless way fiction writers do.

EXERCISE SEVEN

POV

Think up a situation for a narrative sketch of 200–350 words. It can be anything you like, but should involve *several people doing something.* (Several means more than two. More than three will be useful.) It doesn't have to be a big, important event, though it can be; but something should *happen,* even if only a cart-tangle at the supermarket, a wrangle around the table concerning the family division of labor, or a minor street-accident....

Please use little or no dialogue in these POV exercises. While the characters talk, their voices cover the POV, and so you're not exploring that voice, which is the point of the exercise.

Part One: Two Voices

First: Tell your little story from a single POV — that of a participant in the event — an old man, a child, a cat, whatever you like. Use limited third person.

Second: *Retell the same story* from the POV of one of the other people involved in it. Again, use limited third person.

As we go on into the next parts of this exercise, if your little scene or situation or story runs dry, invent another one along the same lines. But if the original one seems to keep turning up new possibilities in different voices, just go on exploring them through it. That will be the most useful, informative way to do the exercise.

Part Two: Detached Narrator

Tell the same story using the detached author or "fly on the wall" POV.

Part Three: Observer-Narrator

If there wasn't a character in the original version who was there but was not a participant, only an onlooker, add such a character now. Tell the same story in that character's voice, in first or third person.

Part Four: Involved Author
Tell the same or a new story using the involved author POV.

Part Four may require you to expand the whole thing, up to two or three pages, 1,000 words or so. You may find you need to give it a context, find out what led up to it, or follow it further. The detached author takes up as little room as possible, but the involved author needs a fair amount of time and space to move around in.

If your original story simply doesn't lend itself to this voice, find a story you want to tell that you can be emotionally and morally involved in. I don't mean by that that it has to be factually true (if it is, you may have trouble getting out of the autobiographical mode into the involved author's voice, which is a *fictional* mode). And I don't mean that you should use your story to preach. I do mean that the story should be about something that concerns you.

Because omniscience is out of fashion, and some readers aren't used to a narrator who admits to knowing the whole story, I thought it might be useful to offer some examples of the involved authorial POV.

Two of them are Victorian, with all the excesses and all the vitality of the shamelessly engaged narrator. This paragraph from *Uncle Tom's Cabin* describes the slave Eliza running away, having learned that her child is to be sold.

EXAMPLE

10

Harriet Beecher Stowe: from *Uncle Tom's Cabin*

The frosty ground creaked beneath her feet, and she trembled at the sound; every quaking leaf and fluttering shadow sent the blood backward to her heart, and quickened her footsteps. She wondered within herself at the strength that seemed to be come upon her; for she felt the weight of her boy as if it had been a feather, and every flutter of fear seemed to increase the supernatural power that bore her on, while from her pale lips burst forth, in frequent ejaculations, the prayer to a Friend above — "Lord, help! Lord, save me!"

If it were *your* Harry, mother, or your Willie, that were going to be torn from you by a brutal trader, tomorrow morning, — if you had seen the man, and heard that the papers were signed and delivered, and you had only from twelve o'clock till morning to make good your escape, — how fast could *you* walk? How many miles could you make in those few brief hours, with the darling at your bosom, — the little sleepy head on your shoulder, — the small, soft arms trustingly holding on to your neck?

The power of such scenes is of course cumulative, but even in this fragment I find the author's sudden turn to the reader startling and moving — "How fast could *you* walk?"

Example Eleven is the first pages of the first three chapters of Dickens's *Bleak House*. The first two chapters are in the involved authorial voice, present tense; the third is in the first person, past tense, the narrator being the character Esther Summerson. The chapters alternate this way throughout the book — an unusual alternation, which I'll talk more about later.

EXAMPLE

11

Charles Dickens: from *Bleak House*

CHAPTER I: IN CHANCERY

LONDON. Michaelmas Term lately over, and the Lord Chancellor sitting in Lincoln's Inn Hall. Implacable November weather. As much mud in the streets, as if the waters had but newly retired from the face of the earth, and it would not be wonderful to meet a Megalosaurus, forty feet long or so, waddling like an elephantine lizard up Holborn Hill. Smoke lowering down from chimney-pots, making a soft black drizzle, with flakes of soot in it as big as full-grown snow-flakes — gone into mourning, one might imagine, for the death of the sun. Dogs, undistinguishable in mire. Horses scarcely better; splashed to their very blinkers. Foot passengers, jostling one another's umbrellas, in a general infection of ill-temper, and losing their foothold at street-corners, where tens of thousands of other foot passengers have been slipping and sliding since the day broke (if this day ever broke), adding new deposits to the crust upon crust of mud, sticking at those points tenaciously to the pavement, and accumulating at compound interest.

Fog everywhere. Fog up the river, where it flows among green aits and meadows; fog down the river, where it rolls defiled among the tiers of shipping, and the water-side pollutions of a great (and dirty) city. Fog on the Essex marshes; fog on the Kentish heights. Fog creeping into the cabooses of collier-brigs; fog lying out on the yards, and hovering in the rigging of great ships; fog drooping on the gunwales of barges and small boats. Fog in the eyes and throats of ancient Greenwich pensioners, wheezing by the firesides of their wards; fog in the stem and bowl of the afternoon pipe of the wrathful skipper, down in his close cabin; fog cruelly pinching the toes and fingers of his shivering little 'prentice boy on deck. Chance people on the bridges peeping over the parapets into a nether sky of fog, with fog all round them, as if they were up in a balloon, and hanging in the misty clouds.

Gas looming through the fog in divers places in the streets, much as the sun may, from the spongy fields, be seen to loom by husbandman and ploughboy. Most of the shops lighted two hours before their time — as the gas seems to know, for it has a haggard and unwilling look.

The raw afternoon is rawest, and the dense fog is densest, and the muddy streets are muddiest, near that leaden-headed old obstruction, appropriate ornament for the threshold of a leaden-headed old corporation: Temple Bar. And hard by Temple Bar, in Lincoln's Inn Hall, at the very heart of the fog, sits the Lord High Chancellor in his High Court of Chancery.

Chapter II: In Fashion

My Lady Dedlock has returned to her house in town for a few days previous to her departure for Paris, where her ladyship intends to stay some weeks; after which her movements are uncertain. The fashionable intelligence says so, for the comfort of the Parisians, and it knows all fashionable things. To know things otherwise, were to be unfashionable. My Lady Dedlock has been down at what she calls, in familiar conversation, her "place" in Lincolnshire. The waters are out in Lincolnshire. An arch of the bridge in the park has been sapped and sopped away. The adjacent low-lying ground, for half a mile in breadth, is a stagnant river, with melancholy trees for islands in it, and a surface punctured all over, all day long, with falling rain. My Lady Dedlock's "place" has been extremely dreary. The weather, for many a day and night, has been so wet that the trees seem wet through, and the soft loppings and prunings of the woodman's axe can make no crash or crackle as they fall. The deer, looking soaked, leave quagmires, where they pass. The shot of a rifle loses its sharpness in the moist air, and its smoke moves in a tardy little cloud towards the green rise, coppice-topped, that makes a background for the falling rain. The view from my Lady Dedlock's own windows is alternately a lead-colored view, and a view in Indian ink. The vases on the stone terrace in the foreground catch the rain all day; and the heavy drops fall, drip, drip, drip, upon the broad flagged pavement, called, from old time, the Ghost's Walk, all night. On Sundays, the little church in the park is mouldy; the oaken pulpit breaks out into a cold sweat; and there is a general smell and taste as of the ancient Dedlocks in their graves. My Lady Dedlock (who is childless), looking out in the early twilight from her boudoir at a keeper's lodge, and seeing the light of a fire upon the latticed panes, and smoke rising from the chimney, and a child, chased by a woman, running out into the rain to meet the shining figure of a wrapped-up man coming through the gate, has been put quite out of temper. My Lady Dedlock says she has been "bored to death."

Therefore my Lady Dedlock has come away from the place in Lincolnshire, and has left it to the rain, and the crows, and the rabbits, and the deer, and the partridges and pheasants. The pictures of the Dedlocks past and gone have seemed to vanish into the damp walls in mere lowness of spirits, as the housekeeper has passed along the old rooms, shutting up the shutters. And when they will next come forth again, the fashionable intelligence — which, like the fiend, is omniscient of the past and present, but not the future — cannot yet undertake to say.

Sir Leicester Dedlock is only a baronet, but there is no mightier baronet than he. His family is as old as the hills, and infinitely more respectable. He has a general opinion that the world might get on without hills, but would be done up without Dedlocks. He would on the whole admit Nature to be a good idea (a little low, perhaps, when not enclosed with a park-fence), but an idea dependent for its execution on your great county families. He is a gentleman of strict conscience, disdainful of all littleness and meanness, and ready, on the shortest notice, to die any death you may please to mention rather than give occasion for the least impeachment of his integrity. He is an honorable, obstinate, truthful, high-spirited, intensely prejudiced, perfectly unreasonable man.

Chapter III: A Progress

I have a great deal of difficulty in beginning to write my portion of these pages, for I know I am not clever. I always knew that. I can remember, when I was a very little girl indeed, I used to say to my doll, when we were alone together, "Now Dolly, I am not clever, you know very well, and you must be patient with me, like a dear!" And so she used to sit propped up in a great arm-chair, with her beautiful complexion and rosy lips, staring at me — or not so much at me, I think, as at nothing — while I busily stitched away, and told her every one of my secrets.

My dear old doll! I was such a shy little thing that I seldom dared to open my lips, and never dared to open my heart, to anybody else. It almost makes me cry to think what a relief it used to be to me, when I came home from school of a day, to run up-stairs to my room, and say, "O you dear faithful Dolly, I knew you would be expecting me!" and then to sit down on the floor, leaning on the elbow of her great chair, and tell her all I had noticed since we parted. I had always rather a noticing way — not a quick way, O no! — a silent way of noticing what passed before me, and thinking I should like to understand it better. I have not by any means a quick understanding. When I love a person very tenderly indeed, it seems to brighten. But even that may be my vanity.

I was brought up, from my earliest remembrance —
like some of the princesses in the fairy stories, only I
was not charming — by my godmother. At least I only
knew her as such. She was a good, good woman! She
went to church three times every Sunday, and to
morning prayers on Wednesdays and Fridays, and to
lectures whenever there were lectures; and never
missed. She was handsome; and if she had ever
smiled, would have been (I used to think) like an angel
— but she never smiled. She was always grave and
strict. She was so very good herself, I thought, that the
badness of other people made her frown all her life. I
felt so different from her, even making every allowance
for the differences between a child and a woman; I felt
so poor, so trifling, and so far off; that I never could be
unrestrained with her — no, could never even love her
as I wished. It made me very sorry to consider how
good she was, and how unworthy of her I was; and I
used ardently to hope that I might have a better heart;
and I talked it over very often with the dear old doll;
but I never loved my godmother as I ought to have
loved her, and as I felt I must have loved her if I had
been a better girl.

Example Twelve, a bit from *The Lord of the Rings*, gives a
charming glimpse of the range open to the involved author, who
can drop into the POV of a passing fox. The fox "never found out
any more about it," and we never find out any more about the
fox; but there he is, alert and alive, all in one moment, watching
for us the obscure beginning of a great adventure.

EXAMPLE

12

J.R.R. Tolkien: from *The Lord of the Rings*

"I am so sleepy," he said, "that soon I shall fall down
on the road. Are you going to sleep on your legs? It is
nearly midnight."

"I thought you liked walking in the dark," said
Frodo. "But there is no great hurry. Merry expects us
some time the day after tomorrow; but that leaves us
nearly two days more. We'll halt at the first likely
spot."

"The wind's in the West," said Sam. "If we get to the
other side of this hill, we shall find a spot that is
sheltered and snug enough, sir. There is a dry fir-
wood just ahead, if I remember rightly." Sam knew the
land well within twenty miles of Hobbiton, but that
was the limit of his geography.

Just over the top of the hill they came on the patch
of fir-wood. Leaving the road they went into the deep
resin-scented darkness of the trees, and gathered
dead sticks and cones to make a fire. Soon they had a
merry crackle of flame at the foot of a large fir-tree
and they sat round it for a while, until they began to
nod. Then, each in an angle of the great tree's roots,
they curled up in their cloaks and blankets, and were
soon fast asleep. They set no watch; even Frodo
feared no danger yet, for they were still in the heart of
the Shire. A few creatures came and looked at them
when the fire had died away. A fox passing through
the wood on business of his own stopped several
minutes and sniffed.

"Hobbits!" he thought. "Well, what next? I have
heard of strange doings in this land, but I have seldom
heard of a hobbit sleeping out of doors under a tree.
Three of them! There's something mighty queer
behind this." He was quite right, but he never found
out any more about it.

If you go back to Example Eight, from the "Time Passes" section of *To the Lighthouse*, you'll see the involved author moving in and out of her own perceptions and characters' points of view so swiftly and so easily that the points of view dissolve into one another and into a voice which is the "voice of the beauty of the world," but which is also the voice of the book itself, the story telling itself. This kind of quick, unsignalled shifting, discussed further below, is rare, and takes immense certainty and skill.

Further Reading

The involved author or "omniscient" author: I'm a little shy about telling anybody to go read Tolstoy's *War and Peace*, since it's quite an undertaking; but it is a wonderful book. And from the technical aspect, it's almost miraculous in the way it shifts imperceptibly from the author's voice to the point of view of a character, speaking with perfect simplicity in the inner voice of a man, a woman, even a hunting dog, and then back to the thoughts of the author...till by the end you feel you have lived many lives: which is perhaps the greatest gift a novel can give.

The detached narrator or "fly on the wall": Any of the writers who called themselves "minimalist," such as Raymond Carver, wrote stories that provide good examples of this technique.

The observer-narrator: Henry James and Willa Cather both used this device frequently. James used limited third person for his observer-narrators, which distances the whole story. Cather used a male witness-narrator in the first person, notably in *My Ántonia* and *A Lost Lady*, and it is interesting to speculate on why a woman writer might speak through a male mask.

The unreliable narrator: Henry James's "The Turn of the Screw" is a classic example. We'd better not believe everything the governess tells us, and we must look through what she says for what she leaves out. Is she deceiving us, or herself?

Point of view in genre fiction is interesting. One might expect most science fiction to be written "omnisciently," without getting inside the characters, but if you read it you'll find this is not true at all. Quite unpretentious series-novels, such as those that use the characters from *Star Trek*, may be highly sophisticated in their frequent changes of POV.

Many mysteries are written "omnisciently," but the limitation and development of the narrator's knowledge is often the central device of a mystery, and many of the finest, like Tony Hillerman's Southwestern or Donna Leon's Venetian or Sara Paretsky's Chicago mysteries, are told from the viewpoint of the detective.

Romances are conventionally told in limited third person, through the perceptions of the heroine, but first person, observer-narrator, and involved author narration are equally suited to the genre.

A founding classic of the Western novel, Owen Wister's *The Virginian*, is mostly told in the first person by an Eastern green-horn observer-narrator (and many later writers in the genre imitated this ploy). Wister switches, a little awkwardly, into the involved author mode to tell us events that the observer-narrator couldn't have observed. Molly Gloss's beautiful Western novel *The Jump-Off Creek* moves back and forth between first person in diary entries and limited third person. An interesting example of personal memoir told in letters — and at one very painful point told in the third person, as if it were about someone other than the author — is Elinore Pruitt Stewart's *Letters of a Woman Homesteader*.

Changing the point of view, using various narrators, is an essential structural device of many modern stories and novels. Margaret Atwood does it wonderfully; look at *The Robber Bride*, or her short stories, or *Alias Grace* (a novel so well made and well written that it could serve as a model for almost any topic in this book). Did you ever read or see the film of *Rashomon?* It's the classic tale of four witnesses telling four utterly different versions of the same event. *Making History*, by Carolyn See, is told in the voices of a set of narrators whose differing voices are an essential part of the book's wit and power. In my novella "Hernes" in *Searoad*, four women tell the story of a small-town family through the whole twentieth century, their voices passing back and forth among the generations. Perhaps the masterpiece of this kind of "choral" narration is *The Waves* by Virginia Woolf.

 *Opinion Piece
on Characters Thinking*

Many writers worry about how to present characters' unspoken thoughts. Editors are likely to put thoughts into italics if you don't stop them.

Thoughts are handled exactly like dialogue, if you present them directly:

"Heavens," Aunt Jane thought, "he's eating that grommet!"

But in presenting characters' thoughts you don't have to use quotation marks, and I think using italics or any typographical device overemphasizes the material. Just make it clear that this bit is going on inside somebody's head. Ways of doing so are various:

As soon as she heard Jim shout, Aunt Jane knew Fred had swallowed the grommet after all.

I just know he's going to swallow that grommet again, Jane said to herself as she sorted buttons.

Oh, Jane thought, I do wish the old fool would hurry up and swallow that grommet!

In critiquing these exercises in point of view, and in thinking and talking about them later, various strong preferences for certain voices and points of view may come out; it can be interesting to consider and discuss them.

Later on, you may want to return to some of these exercises, using the instructions on a different story, perhaps recombining the exercises. The choice of point(s) of view, the voice in which one narrates one's story, can make an immense difference to the tone, the effect, even the meaning of the story. Writers often find that a story they want to tell "sticks" and won't go right until they find the right person to tell it — whether it's a choice between first and third person, or between the involved author and a limited third-person narrator, or between a character involved in the action and a bystander, or between one and several narrators. The following optional exercises might help bring out the wealth of choices, and the necessity of choosing.

Tell a different story, with both versions in the first person instead of limited third.

Or tell the story of an accident twice: once in the detached author mode, or in a journalistic, reportorial voice; then from the viewpoint of a character involved in the accident.

If there's a mode or voice you don't particularly like, that's probably the one you should try again, if only to find out why you dislike it. (I'm sure you'll like your tapioca if you'll just try it, dear.)

They sailed easily from the past to the present,

but now

they can't get back.

EIGHT

CHANGING POINT OF VIEW

OU CAN CHANGE POINT OF VIEW, OF COURSE. IT IS YOUR GODGIVEN right as an American fiction writer. All I'm saying is, you need to know that you're doing it; some American fiction writers don't. And you need to know when and how to do it, so that when you shift, you carry the reader effortlessly with you.

Shifting between first and third person, as in the "Another Additional Option" to Exercise Six, is enormously difficult in a short piece. Even in a novel, like Example Eleven, this shift is uncommon, and may be, in the end, unwise. *Bleak House* is a powerful novel, and some of its dramatic power may come from this highly artificial alternation and contrast of voices. But the transition from Dickens to Esther is always a jolt. And the twenty-year-old girl sometimes begins to sound awfully like the middle-aged novelist, which is implausible, though rather a relief, because Esther is given to tiresome fits of self-deprecation, and Dickens isn't. Dickens was well aware of the dangers of his narrative strategy: the "omniscient" author never overlaps with the observer-narrator, never enters Esther's mind, never sees her. The two narratives remain separate. The plot unites them, but they never touch. It is an odd device.

So my general feeling is — if you try the first-to-third shift, have a really good reason for doing it, and do it with great care. Don't strip your gears.

You really can't shift between detached and involved authorial voice within one piece. I don't know why you'd want to.

And once again: the involved author can move from one viewpoint character to another at will; but if it happens very often, unless the writing is superbly controlled (like Example Six), readers will tire of being jerked from mind to mind, or will lose track of whose mind they're supposed to be in.

Particularly disturbing is the effect of being jerked into a different viewpoint *for a moment*. The narrative is being told from inside Aunt Jane's viewpoint. Then for one sentence we're in Uncle Fred's viewpoint. Then we snap back into Jane's. With care, the involved author can do this (Tolkien does it with the fox). But it *cannot* be done in limited third person. Remember when Della raised her violet eyes? That was a *one-word* POV shift. It doesn't work.

Involved author and limited third person have a wide overlap, since the involved author can and usually does use third-person narration freely, and may limit perception for some while to a single person. When the authorial voice is subtle, it can be hard to say for sure which mode a piece is written in.

So: you can shift from one viewpoint character to another any time you like, if you know why and how you're doing it, if you're cautious about doing it frequently, and if you never do it momentarily.

CHANGING VOICES

Version One: Quick Shifts in Limited Third

A short narrative, 300–600 words. You can use one of the sketches from Exercise Seven, or make up a new scene of the same kind: several people involved in the same activity or event.

Tell the story, *using several different view-point characters (narrators) in limited third person*, changing from one to another as the narrative proceeds.

Mark the changes with line breaks, with the narrator's name in parentheses at the head of that section, or with any device you like.

I keep saying that shifting POV frequently and without no-tice is risky, dangerous. So you want to do something dangerous.

Version Two: Thin Ice

In 300–1,000 words. Tell the same or a new story of the same kind, deliberately shifting POV from character to character several times without any obvious signal to the reader that you're doing so.

You can of course do Version Two merely by removing the "signals" from Version

One, but you won't learn much by doing so. "Thin Ice" calls for a different narrative technique, and possibly a different narrative. I think it is likely to end up being written by the involved author, even though you are apparently using only limited third-person viewpoint. This ice really is thin, and the waters are deep.

A model of this kind of POV shifting is Example Thirteen, from *To the Lighthouse*.

EXAMPLE

13

Virginia Woolf: from *To the Lighthouse*

What brought her to say that: "We are in the hands of the Lord?" she wondered. The insincerity slipping in among the truths roused her, annoyed her. She returned to her knitting again. How could any Lord have made this world? she asked. With her mind she had always seized the fact that there is no reason, order, justice: but suffering, death, the poor. There was no treachery too base for the world to commit; she knew that. No happiness lasted; she knew that. She knitted with firm composure, slightly pursing her lips and, without being aware of it, so stiffened and composed the lines of her face in a habit of sternness that when her husband passed, though he was chuckling at the thought that Hume, the philosopher, grown enormously fat, had stuck in a bog, he could not help noting, as he passed, the sternness at the heart of her beauty. It saddened him, and her remoteness pained him, and he felt, as he passed, that he could not protect her, and, when he reached the hedge, he was sad. He could do nothing to help her. He must stand by and watch her. Indeed, the infernal truth was, he made things worse for her. He was irritable — he was touchy. He had lost his temper over the Lighthouse. He looked into the hedge, into its intricacy, its darkness.

Always, Mrs. Ramsay felt, one helped oneself out of solitude reluctantly by laying hold of some little odd or end, some sound, some sight. She listened, but it was all very still; cricket was over; the children were in their baths; there was only the sound of the sea. She stopped knitting; she held the long reddish-brown stocking dangling in her hands a moment. She saw the light again. With some irony in her interrogation, for when one woke at all, one's relations changed, she looked at the steady light, the pitiless, the remorseless, which was so much her, yet so little her, which had her at its beck and call (she woke in the night and saw it bent across their bed, stroking the floor), but for all that she thought, watching it with fascination, hypnotised, as if it were stroking with its silver fingers some sealed vessel in her brain whose bursting would flood her with delight, she had known happiness, exquisite happiness, intense happiness, and it silvered the rough waves a little more brightly, as daylight faded, and the blue went out of the sea and it rolled in waves of pure lemon which curved and swelled and broke upon the beach and the ecstasy burst in her eyes and waves of pure delight raced over the floor of her mind and she felt, It is enough! It is enough!

He turned and saw her. Ah! She was lovely, lovelier now than ever he thought. But he could not speak to her. He could not interrupt her. He wanted urgently to speak to her now that James was gone and she was alone at last. But he resolved, no; he would not interrupt her. She was aloof from him now in her beauty, in her sadness. He would let her be, and he passed her without a word, though it hurt him that she should look so distant, and he could not reach her, he could do nothing to help her. And again he would have passed her without a word had she not, at that very moment, given him of her own free will what she knew he would never ask, and called to him and taken the green shawl off the picture frame, and gone to him. For he wished, she knew, to protect her.

Notice how Woolf makes the transitions effortlessly but perfectly clearly. From "What brought her to say that" to the second "she knew that," we are in Mrs. Ramsay's POV; then we slip out of it, the signal being that *we can see Mrs. Ramsay* slightly pursing her lips, composing her face "in a habit of sternness," which Mr. Ramsay, passing, chuckling at the thought of a philosopher stuck in a bog, *sees from his POV;* and he grows sad, feeling that he cannot protect her. The paragraph indent is the signal for the switch back to Mrs. Ramsay. What are the next switches, and how are they signalled?

A Reminder-Note About Imitation

A rational fear of plagiarizing, and an individualistic valuation of originality, have stopped many prose writers from using deliberate imitation as a learning tool. In poetry courses, students may be asked to write "in the manner of" so-and-so, or to use a stanza or a cadence from a published poet as a model, but teachers of prose writing seem to shun the very idea of imitating. I think conscious, deliberate imitation of a piece of prose one admires can be good training, a means towards finding one's own voice as a narrative writer. If you want to imitate any of the examples in this book, or anything else, do so. What is essential is the consciousness. When imitating, it's necessary to remember the work, however successful, is practice, not an end in itself, but a means towards the end of writing with skill and freedom in one's own voice.

In critiquing these exercises, you might talk about how well the shifts work, what's gained (or lost?) by them, how the piece might have differed if told from one POV only.

For a while afterward, when reading fiction, you might take a moment to consider what POV is being used, who the viewpoint character is, when the POV shifts, and so on. It's interesting to see how different writers do it, and you can learn a great deal from watching great artists of narrative technique such as Woolf and Atwood.

A: *Lower the topgallants!*

B: *I will when I find them.*

NINE

INDIRECT NARRATION, OR WHAT TELLS

*T*HIS SECTION HAS TO DO WITH VARIOUS ASPECTS OF STORYTELLING that don't seem to be storytelling in the obvious sense of recounting events.

Some people interpret story to mean plot. Some reduce story to action. Plot is so much discussed in literature and writing courses, and action is so highly valued, that I want to put in a counterweight opinion.

A story that has nothing but action and plot is a pretty poor affair; and some great stories have neither. To my mind, plot is merely one way of telling a story, by connecting the happenings tightly, usually through causal chains. Plot is a marvelous device. But it's not superior to story, and not even necessary to it. As for action, indeed a story must move, something must happen; but the action can be nothing more than a letter sent that doesn't arrive, a thought unspoken, the passage of a summer day. Unceasing violent action is usually a sign that there is, in fact, no story being told.

In E.M. Forster's *Aspects of the Novel*, which I've loved and argued with for years, is a famous illustration of story: "The king died and then the queen died." And plot: "The king died and then the queen died of grief."

My opinion is that those are both rudimentary stories, the first loose, the second slightly structured. Neither one has or is a plot. "When the king's brother murdered the king and married the queen, the crown prince was upset" — now there's a plot; one you may recognize, in fact.

There is a limited number of plots (some say seven, some say twelve, some say thirty). There is no limit to the number of stories. Everybody in the world has their story, and every meeting of one with another begins another story. Somebody asked Willie Nelson where he got his songs, and he said, "The air's full of melodies, you just reach out...." The world's full of stories, you just reach out.

I say this in an attempt to unhook people from the idea that they have to make an elaborate plan of a tight plot before they're allowed to write a story. If that's the way you like to write, write that way, of course. But if it isn't, if you aren't a planner or a plotter, don't worry. The world's full of stories.... All you need may be a character or two, or a conversation, or a situation, or a place, and you'll find the story there. You think about it, you work it out at least partly before you start writing, so that you know in a general way where you're going, but the rest works itself out in the telling. I like my image of "steering the craft," but in fact the story boat is a magic one. It knows its course. The job of the person at the helm is to help it find its own way to wherever it's going.

In this section we're also dealing with how to provide information in a narrative.

This is a skill science fiction and fantasy writers are keenly aware of, because they often have a great deal of information to convey that the reader has no way of knowing unless told. If my story's set in Chicago in 1995, I can assume that my readers have some general idea of the time and place and how things work there, and can fill in the picture from the barest hints. But if my story's set on 4-Beta Draconis in 3295, my readers have no idea what to expect. The world of the story must be created and explained in the story. This is part of the particular interest and beauty of science fiction and fantasy: writer and reader collaborate in world-making. But it's a tricky business.

If the information is poured out as a lecture, barely concealed by some stupid device — "Oh, Captain, do tell me how the antimatter dissimulator works!" and then he does, endlessly — we have what science fiction writers call an Expository Lump. Crafty writers (in any genre) don't allow Exposition to form Lumps. They break up the information, grind it fine, and make it into bricks to build the story with.

Almost all narrative carries some load of explaining and describing. This expository freight can be as much a problem in memoir as it is in science fiction. Making the information part of the story is a learnable skill. As always, a good part of the solution consists simply in being aware that there is a problem.

So in this section we're dealing with stories that tell us things without appearing to be telling us. We're practicing invisible exposition.

The first exercise in this section is a stark and simple one.

▲Exercise Nine: Part 1

TELLING IT SLANT

Part One: A & B

The goal of this exercise is to tell a story and present two characters through dialogue alone.

Write a page or two — word count would be misleading, as dialogue leaves a lot of unfilled lines — a page or two of pure dialogue.

Write it like a play, with A and B as the characters' names. No stage directions. No description of the characters. *Nothing* but what A says and what B says. Everything the reader knows about who they are, where they are, and what's going on, comes through what they say.

If you want a suggestion for the topic, put two people into some kind of crisis situation: the car just ran out of gas; the space ship is about to crash; the doctor has just realized that the old man she's treating for a heart attack is her father....

Note: "A & B" is not an exercise in writing a short story. It's an exercise in one of the *elements* of storytelling. You may, in fact, come out with a quite satisfactory little playlet or performance piece, but the technique is not one to use much or often in narrative prose.

Critiquing: If you're working in a group, this is a good one to write in class. You'll probably find that people mutter a good deal as they write it.

If the text's clear enough for another person to read, when you come to reading it aloud it's good fun for the author to be A and somebody else to be B (after a silent read-through.) If you're very brave, give your piece to *two* other people to read aloud. If they're pretty good readers, you may learn a good deal about how to fix it from how they read it, noticing where they stumble or mistake the emphasis, and how natural or "stagey" it sounds.

If you're working by yourself, read it out loud. Not whispering. OUT LOUD.

In discussion or thinking about it, you may want to consider the effectiveness of the device as such (it is a tiny drama, after all). You might also think about these matters: Is the story clear? Do we learn enough about the people and the situation — do we need more information? Or less? What do we in fact know about the people (for example, do we know their gender)? What do we feel about them? Could we tell the two voices apart without the A and B signals, and if not, how might they be more differentiated? Do people actually talk this way?

Later on: "A & B" is a permanently useful exercise, like "Chastity." If you haven't anything better to do you can always stick A and B in the car in the middle of Nevada, or whatever, and see what they say. Do remember, though, that unless you're a playwright, the result isn't what you want; it's only an element of what you want. Actors embody and re-create the words of drama. In fiction, a tremendous amount of story and character may be given through the dialogue, but the story-world and its people have to be created by the storyteller. If there's nothing in it but disembodied voices, too much is missing.

Polyphony

All the same, I'm going on with voices for a while.

One of the marvelous things about that marvelous thing the novel is its many-voicedness, its polyphony. All kinds of people get to think, feel, and talk in a novel, and that great psychological variety is a part of the vitality and beauty of the form.

It might seem that the writer needs a gift of mimicry, like an impersonator, to achieve this variety of voices. But it isn't that. It's more like what a serious actor does, sinking self in character-self. It's a willingness to be the characters, letting what they think and say rise from inside them. It's a willingness to share control with one's creation.

Writers may need conscious practice in writing in voices that aren't their own; they may, in fact, resist it.

Some who write memoir write only in one voice, their own.

If all the people in the memoir say only what the author wanted to hear, all we hear is the author speaking — an interminable monologue. Some fiction writers do the same thing. They use their characters as mouthpieces for what they want to say or hear. And so you get the story where everybody talks alike, and they all talk like the author.

What's needed in this case is conscious and serious practice in hearing, and using, and being used by, other people's voices.

Instead of talking, let other people talk through you.

I can't tell a memoir writer how to do this, because I don't know how to listen for a real voice and reproduce it truly. It's not a skill I ever practiced. I admire it in awe. Perhaps one way to begin practicing it would be to listen to people on the bus, in the supermarket, in the waiting room, and try to remember and write down their talk later, as a private exercise in fidelity to real voice.

If you're a fiction writer, though, I can tell you how to let people talk through you. Listen. Just be quiet, and listen. Let the character talk. Don't censor, don't control. Listen, and write.

Don't be afraid of doing this. After all, you *are* in control. These characters are entirely dependent on you. You made them up. Let the poor fictive creatures have their say — you can hit delete any time you like.

Exercise Nine: Part 2

Part Two: Being the Stranger

Write a narrative of 200–600 words, a scene involving at least two people and some kind of action or event.

Use a single viewpoint character, either in first person or limited third person, who is involved in the event. Give us the character's thoughts and feelings in their own words.

The viewpoint character (real or invented) is to be somebody you dislike, or disapprove of, or hate, or feel to be extremely different from yourself.

The situation might be a quarrel between neighbors, or a relative's visit, or somebody acting weird at the checkout counter — whatever will show the viewpoint character being who they are, doing what they do.

To think about before writing: When I say "the stranger," "someone extremely different from yourself," I mean it in the psychological sense: somebody you don't empathize or sympathize with easily.

A person who is profoundly different from you socially, culturally, by language, by nation, may in fact not be accessible to you as a character. You may really not know enough about their life to write about them from inside. My advice is, stick close to home. There are strangers everywhere.

For some writers who have never practised this sort of psychological displacement, it can be hard and scary just to change gender — to write as a person of the opposite sex. If this applies to you, do it.

Many young writers have never tried to write as an old person ("old" may mean forty). If this applies to you, do it.

Many writers, even old ones, write of family relationships always as the child, never as a parent. If this applies to you, try writing as one of the parental, not the child, generation.

If you usually write about a certain kind of person, write about a totally different kind of person.

If you mostly write fiction, you might make this an exercise in memoir. Revive a memory of a person you have disliked, or held in contempt, or felt to be very alien to you. Describe some moment you recall, from that person's POV, trying to guess how they felt, what they saw, why they said what they said. How did they perceive you?

If you mostly write memoir, you might make this an exercise in fiction. Invent a person who is truly different from yourself, who's not sympathetic to you. Get inside that person's skin, think and feel as they do.

Note: If you're recalling actual events, don't use this exercise to rouse up sleeping demons. It's not therapy. It's just an exercise, though it's in an important aspect of writing, which does demand a certain courage of the writer.

You can use this exercise satirically, hatefully, showing us how awful the viewpoint character is by exposing what they really think and feel. That is a legitimate and canny writing tactic. But it defeats the purpose of the exercise, which is to *suspend your judgment* on this person. What the exercise asks of you is "to walk a mile in their moccasins," seeing the world through their eyes.

In critiquing, you might use this last suggestion as a criterion. As readers, are we really inside the viewpoint character, so that we understand something about how they see the world, or did the writer stay outside, sitting in judgment, trying to force us to make the same judgment? If there's spitefulness, vindictiveness, in the piece, whose is it? — Another approach: Is the voice the piece is told in a convincing one? Are there particular places where it rings false or rings true? Can you discuss (with others or with yourself) why this is so?

Thinking about it afterwards, you might consider why you chose the person you chose as the viewpoint character. And you might consider whether you found out anything about yourself *as a writer,* about your way of handling characters. Will you try again to write in a voice very different from your own?

Now to get away from voices entirely for a while.

Part Three of Exercise Nine is just like Part One, except it's the opposite. In "A & B" you had nothing but voices to work with, no scenery at all. In this one you have nothing to work with but the scenery. Nobody's there, and nothing — apparently — is happening.

Before doing this one, you might want to read Examples Fourteen, Fifteen, and Sixteen.

The description of Jacob's room at college is light in tone, seeming not very significant. Yet the name of the book is *Jacob's Room*.... And when we come to the end of that book, on the last page, the last two sentences of this little description are repeated word for word, with an utterly different, heartbreaking resonance. (Oh, the power of repetition!)

EXAMPLE

14

Virginia Woolf: from *Jacob's Room*

The feathery white moon never let the sky grow dark; all night the chestnut blossoms were white in the green; dim was the cow-parsley in the meadows.

The waiters at Trinity must have been shuffling china plates like cards, from the clatter that could be heard in the Great Court. Jacob's rooms, however, were in Neville's Court; at the top; so that reaching his door one went in a little out of breath; but he wasn't there. Dining in Hall, presumably. It will be quite dark in Neville's Court long before midnight, only the pillars opposite will always be white, and the fountains. A curious effect the gate has, like lace upon pale green. Even in the window you hear the plates; a hum of talk, too, from the diners; the Hall lit up, and the swing-doors opening and shutting with a soft thud. Some are late.

Jacob's room had a round table and two low chairs.

There were yellow flags in a jar on the mantelpiece; a photograph of his mother; cards from societies with little raised crescents, coats of arms, and initials; notes and pipes; on the table lay paper ruled with a red margin — an essay, no doubt — "Does History consist of the Biographies of Great Men?" There were books enough; very few French books; but then any one who's worth anything reads just what he likes, as the mood takes him, with extravagant enthusiasm. Lives of the Duke of Wellington, for example; Spinoza; the works of Dickens; the *Faery Queen*; a Greek dictionary with the petals of poppies pressed to silk between the pages; all the Elizabethans. His slippers were incredibly shabby, like boats burnt to the water's rim. Then there were photographs from the Greeks, and a mezzotint from Sir Joshua — all very English. The works of Jane Austen, too, in deference, perhaps, to some one else's standard. Carlyle was a prize. There were books upon the Italian painters of the Renaissance, a *Manual of the Diseases of the Horse*, and all the usual text-books. Listless is the air in an empty room, just swelling the curtain; the flowers in the jar shift. One fibre in the wicker arm-chair creaks, though no one sits there.

This is the famous opening of Hardy's *The Return of the Native*. There are no characters in the first chapter at all, except Egdon Heath. Hardy's prose is circuitous and heavy-footed, and one really needs to read the whole chapter to feel how tremendously he sets the scene. If you go on and read the whole book, the character you may remember most clearly from it, years after, is still Egdon Heath.

EXAMPLE

15

Thomas Hardy: from *The Return of the Native*

A Saturday afternoon in November was approaching
the time of twilight, and the vast tract of unenclosed
wild known as Egdon Heath embrowned itself moment
by moment. Overhead the hollow stretch of whitish
cloud shutting out the sky was as a tent which had
the whole heath for its floor.

The heaven being spread with this pallid screen and
the earth with the darkest vegetation, their meeting-
line at the horizon was clearly marked. In such
contrast the heath wore the appearance of an instal-
ment of night which had taken up its place before its
astronomical hour was come: darkness had to a great
extent arrived hereon, while day stood distinct in the
sky. Looking upwards, a furze-cutter would have been
inclined to continue work; looking down, he would
have decided to finish his faggot and go home. The
distant rims of the world and of the firmament seemed
to be a division in time no less than a division in
matter. The face of the heath by its mere complexion
added half an hour to evening; it could in like manner
retard the dawn, sadden noon, anticipate the frowning
of storms scarcely generated, and intensify the opacity
of a moonless midnight to a cause of shaking and
dread.

In fact, precisely at this transitional point of its
nightly roll into darkness the great and particular
glory of the Egdon waste began, and nobody could be
said to understand the heath who had not been there
at such a time. It could best be felt when it could not
clearly be seen, its complete effect and explanation
lying in this and the succeeding hours before the next
dawn: then, and only then, did it tell its true tale. The
spot was, indeed, a near relation of night, and when
night showed itself an apparent tendency to gravitate

together could be perceived in its shades and the scene. The sombre stretch of rounds and hollows seemed to rise and meet the evening gloom in pure sympathy, the heath exhaling darkness as rapidly as the heavens precipitated it. And so the obscurity in the air and the obscurity in the land closed together in a black fraternization towards which each advanced half-way.

The place became full of a watchful intentness now; for when other things sank brooding to sleep the heath appeared slowly to awake and listen. Every night its Titanic form seemed to await something; but it had waited thus, unmoved, during so many centuries, through the crises of so many things, that it could only be imagined to await one last crisis — the final overthrow.

We follow Jane Eyre in her first tour of Thornfield Hall. These rooms aren't empty, as Jane and the housekeeper pass through them talking; but the power of the piece is in the description of the furnishings, the rooftop and its wide bright view, the sudden return to the dim passages of the third storey, and then the laugh Jane hears. "It was a curious laugh; distinct, formal, mirthless." (Oh, the power of the right adjectives!)

EXAMPLE

16

Charlotte Brontë: from *Jane Eyre*

When we left the dining-room, she proposed to show me over the rest of the house; and I followed her upstairs and downstairs, admiring as I went; for all was well arranged and handsome. The large front chambers I thought especially grand: and some of the third-storey rooms, though dark and low, were interesting from their air of antiquity. The furniture once appropriated to the lower apartments had from time to time been removed here, as fashions changed: and the imperfect light entering by their narrow casement showed bedsteads of a hundred years old; chests in oak or walnut, looking, with their strange carvings of palm branches and cherubs' heads, like types of the Hebrew ark; rows of venerable chairs, high-backed and narrow; stools still more antiquated, on whose cushioned tops were yet apparent traces of half-effaced embroideries, wrought by fingers that for two generations had been coffin-dust. All these relics gave to the third storey of Thornfield Hall the aspect of a home of the past: a shrine of memory. I liked the hush, the gloom, the quaintness of these retreats in the day; but I by no means coveted a night's repose on one of those wide and heavy beds: shut in, some of them, with doors of oak; shaded, others, with wrought old English hangings crusted with thick work, portraying effigies of strange flowers, and stranger birds, and strangest human beings, — all which would have looked strange, indeed, by the pallid gleam of moonlight.

"Do the servants sleep in these rooms?" I asked.

"No; they occupy a range of smaller apartments to the back; no one ever sleeps here: one would almost say that, if there were a ghost at Thornfield Hall, this would be its haunt."

"So I think: you have no ghost, then?"

"None that I ever heard of," returned Mrs. Fairfax, smiling.

"Nor any traditions of one? no legends or ghost stories?"

"I believe not. And yet it is said the Rochesters have been rather a violent than a quiet race in their time: perhaps, though, that is the reason they rest tranquilly in their graves now."

"Yes — 'after life's fitful fever they sleep well,'" I muttered. "Where are you going now, Mrs. Fairfax?" for she was moving away.

"On to the leads; will you come and see the view from thence?" I followed still, up a very narrow staircase to the attics, and thence by a ladder and through a trap-door to the roof of the hall. I was now on a level with the crow colony, and could see into their nests. Leaning over the battlements and looking far down, I surveyed the grounds laid out like a map: the bright and velvet lawn closely girdling the grey base of the mansion; the field, wide as a park, dotted with its ancient timber; the wood, dun and sere, divided by a path visibly overgrown, greener with moss than the trees were with foliage; the church at the gates, the road, the tranquil hills, all reposing in the autumn day's sun; the horizon bounded by a propitious sky, azure, marbled with pearly white. No feature in the scene was extraordinary, but all was pleasing. When I turned from it and repassed the trap-door, I could scarcely see my way down the ladder; the attic seemed black as a vault compared with that arch of blue air to which I had been looking up, and to that sunlit scene of grove, pasture, and green hill, of which the hall was the centre, and over which I had been gazing with delight.

Mrs. Fairfax stayed behind a moment to fasten the trap-door; I, by dint of groping, found the outlet from the attic, and proceeded to descend the narrow garret staircase. I lingered in the long passage to which this led, separating the front and back rooms of the third storey: narrow, low, and dim, with only one little window at the far end, and looking, with its two rows of small black doors all shut, like a corridor in some Bluebeard's castle.

While I paced softly on, the last sound I expected to hear in so still a region, a laugh, struck my ear. It was a curious laugh; distinct, formal, mirthless. I stopped: the sound ceased, only for an instant; it began again, louder: for at first, though distinct, it was very low. It passed off in a clamorous peal that seemed to wake

an echo in every lonely chamber; though it originated
but in one, and I could have pointed out the door
whence the accents issued.

FURTHER READING

All the examples quoted are fairly direct in their description,
yet they do not slow or stop the story. The story is *in* the scene,
in the things described. There's a tendency to fear descriptive
"passages," as if they were unnecessary ornaments that inevitably slow the "action." To see how a landscape and a great deal
of information about people and a way of life can *be* the "action,"
the onward movement of the story, look at Linda Hogan's *Solar
Storms*, Leslie Marmon Silko's *Ceremony*, or Esmeralda Santiago's
memoir, *When I Was Puerto Rican*.

In well-written, serious thrillers, such as John le Carré's *The
Tailor of Panama*, information about their setting, about politics,
and so on, is in the same way integral to the story. Good mysteries are good at conveying information, too, from Dorothy Sayers's
classic *Murder Must Advertise* and *The Nine Tailors* on. In a fantasy
such as Tolkien's *The Lord of the Rings* a whole world is created
and explained, effortlessly and joyously, through a wealth of
vivid, concrete detail, as the story moves unceasingly forward. I
believe there is no moment in that immense book in which the
reader doesn't know exactly where the characters are and what
the weather is doing.

Science fiction, as I said, specializes in getting an immense
amount of information to function as part of the narrative. Vonda
N. McIntyre's *The Moon and the Sun* tells you more about the
splendid court and eccentric courtiers of Louis XIV than many
history books do, and it's all dazzling story.

Good history is all story too — look at Hubert Herring's great
Latin America and marvel at how he worked twenty countries and
five hundred years into a real page-turner. Stephen Jay Gould is
a master at embedding complex scientific information and theory
in strong narrative essays. Memoirists often seem a little old-fashioned in separating description from story; like Walter Scott back
in the early nineteenth century, they show us a scene and then

relate what happened there. But such deeply "placed" books as Mary Austin's *Land of Little Rain*, Isak Dinesen's *Out of Africa*, W.H. Hudson's *The Purple Land*, weave scenery, characters, and emotions into one rich and seamless fabric. In autobiographies such as those by Frederick Douglass, Sarah Winnemucca, Maxine Hong Kingston, Jill Ker Conway, and in masterful biographies such as Winifred Gérin's of the Brontës or Hermione Lee's of Virginia Woolf, the narrative carries effortlessly a wealth of information about the times, the places, the events of a life, which give the story a depth and solidity any novelist may envy.

E X E R C I S E   N I N E :   P A R T   3

Part Three: Implication

Each part of this should involve 200–600 words of descriptive prose. In both, the voice is either involved author or detached author. No viewpoint character.

Character by indirection: Describe a *character* by describing any *place* inhabited or frequented by that character — a room, house, garden, office, studio, bed, whatever. (The character *isn't present at the time.*)

The untold event: Give us a glimpse of the mood and nature of some event or deed by describing the *place* — room, rooftop, street, park, landscape, whatever — where it happened or is about to happen. (The event or deed *doesn't happen in your piece.*)

You aren't to say anything directly about the person, or the event, which is in fact the subject of the piece. This is the stage without the actors on it; this is the camera panning before the action starts. And this kind of suggestion is something words can do better than any other medium, even film.

Use any "props" you like: furniture, clothes, belongings, weather, climate, a period in history, plants, rocks, smells, sounds, anything. Work the Pathetic Fallacy* for all it's worth. Focus on any item or detail that reveals the character, or that suggests what happened or will happen.

Remember, this is a *narrative* device, part of a story. Everything you describe is there in order to further that story. Give us evidences that build up into a consistent, coherent mood or atmosphere, from which we can infer, or glimpse, or intuit, the absent person or the untold act. A mere inventory of articles won't do it, and will bore the reader. Every detail must *tell*.

If you find "Implication" an interesting exercise, you can repeat either or both parts: this time, instead of the authorial voice, use the voice of a character in the story to describe the scene.

Note: In descriptive writing, give a thought from time to time to the *senses other than sight*. Sound, above all, is evocative. We have a limited vocabulary for smell, but mention of a certain scent or stink can set a feeling-tone. Taste and touch are forbidden to the detached author. The involved author can go around telling us how things feel to the hand, though I don't think even an involved author gets to actually eat the fruit that looks so fresh and delicious, or has gotten so mouldy, in the shining, or the dusty, wooden bowl.... But if a character in the story is telling it, all senses can come into play.

OPTIONAL ADDITIONS TO EXERCISE NINE

THE EXPOSITORY LUMP

My workshoppers were interested in the concept of the Expository Lump, as any writer must be, and they wanted an exercise specifically aimed at it. I said I couldn't think of one. They said, "You have to make up some information that we have to work into a narrative." This is a delightful idea. I get to invent this stuff, and you have to do all the hard work.

As my knowledge of the real world is sketchy, I provide a fantasy subject. Don't be afraid; it's just an exercise. You can return to the real world immediately after and forever.

Option One: The Fantastic Lump
Study this piece of false history and invented information till you're quite familiar with it. Then use it as the foundation of a story or a scene. As you write the scene, "compost" the information, break it up, spread it out, slip it into conversation or

action-narration or anywhere you can make it go so it doesn't feel Lumpy. Tell it by implication, by passing reference, by hint, by any means you like. Tell it so that the reader doesn't realize they're learning anything. Include enough of it that the reader can fully understand the situation the queen is in. This will take, I think, two or three pages, possibly more.

The kingdom of Harath has not had a ruler for twenty years, since young King Pell disappeared in a battle on the border of the kingdom with the Ennedi, who are magicians. (The people of Harath have never practiced magic, as their religion declares it to be against the will of the Nine Goddesses.) What became of the king is not known. He left no known heir. (Harath used to be ruled by queens, but since Pell's grandfather's time, men have ruled and women are not permitted to.) Succession to Pell's throne was disputed by various members of the royal line and by a powerful minister, Jussa, who declared himself the Queen's Guardian. Battles between these factions have left the kingdom impoverished and demoralized.

At the time of our story, the Ennedi are again threatening to invade on the eastern border. Jussa is keeping the queen, a woman of forty, imprisoned in a remote tower under the pretext of keeping her safe. In fact he is afraid of her, and alarmed by rumors of a mysterious person who managed to visit her secretly while she was in the palace. This person might be the leader of a rebel faction who is said to be the Queen's illegitimate child, or it might be King Pell, or it might be an Ennedi magician, or....

You take it from there. You don't have to write the whole story, just a scene or two that is based on this information and includes enough of it to be understandable to a reader who has *not* read the information. The tower where the queen is being held might be a good place to start. Use any viewpoint you like. You get to name the queen.

Option Two: The Real Lump

I thought this one up with memoir writers in mind. Because it deals with actual experience, I can't provide the material for you. Think of something you know how to do that involves a complex series of specific actions: for example, making a loaf of bread or a piece of jewelry, building a barn, playing a game of blackjack or a game of polo, sailing a boat, repairing an engine, setting up a conference, setting a broken wrist, setting type.... It should be something that not everybody knows how to do, so that most readers will want some explanation of the procedures.

If nothing comes to mind, find an encyclopedia and look up a process — maybe something you always wondered about — how to make paper by hand, how to bind a book, how to shoe a horse, whatever. You'll have to use your imagination to supply the sensory details that will keep the description vivid. (Industrial processes are almost certainly too complicated to "bone up" this way; but if you already have knowledge of one, there's an excellent subject.)

Write a scene, involving at least two people, in which this process is going on, either in the background of a conversation, or as the locus of the action. Keep the description specific and concrete. Avoid jargon, but if the process has a lingo of its own, use it. Whatever the process is, make the various steps clear to the reader, but don't let it appear to be what the piece is all about.

If we dump the ballast we'll be there in no time.

TEN

CROWDING
AND LEAPING

*A*S THE WORKSHOP WENT ON, I BEGAN TO THINK ABOUT AN ASPECT of narrative technique that I hadn't originally seen clearly. It has to do with what details are included, what omitted. It has to do with focus — the focus of the sentence, the paragraph, the piece as a whole. I call it Crowding and Leaping, because those words describe the process in a physical way, which I like.

Crowding is what Keats meant when he told poets to "load every rift with ore." It's what we mean when we exhort ourselves to avoid flabby language and clichés, never to use ten vague words where two will do, always to seek the vivid phrase, the exact word. By crowding I mean also keeping the story full, always full of what's happening in it; keeping it moving, not slacking and wandering into irrelevancies; keeping it interconnected with itself, rich with echoes forward and backward. Vivid, exact, concrete, accurate, dense, rich: these adjectives describe a prose that is crowded with sensations, meanings, and implications.

But leaping is just as important. What you leap over is what you leave out. And what you leave out is infinitely more than what you leave in. There's got to be white space around the word, silence around the voice. Listing is not describing. Only the relevant belongs. Some say God is in the details; some say the Devil is in the details. Both are correct.

If you try to include everything in a description, you end up like poor "Funes the Memorious" in Borges's story, which, if you have not read, I recommend with all my heart. Overcrowded descriptions clog the story and suffocate themselves. (For an example of a novel choked to death by words, look at *Salammbô* by Gustave Flaubert. Flaubert has been set up as such a universal model, and his *le mot juste*◆ has been made into such a shibboleth, that it's salutary to watch the poor man founder in a quicksand consisting entirely of *mots justes*.)

Tactically speaking, I'd say go ahead and crowd in the first draft — put everything in. Then in revising decide what counts, what tells; and cut and recombine till what's left is what counts. Leap boldly.

Action writers often crowd but fail to leap fast enough or far enough. We've all read descriptions of a fist-fight, or a battle, or a sports event, which by trying to give a blow-by-blow account merely create confusion and boredom. (For a magnificent example of action writing, look at any of the sea battles in Patrick O'Brian's Aubrey-Maturin novels. Everything the reader needs to know is included, but nothing more. At each moment we know exactly where we are and what's happening. Every detail both enriches the picture and speeds the action. The language is transparent. The sensory details are intense, brief, precise. And you can't stop reading till it's over.)

Leaping in narrative is an important skill. Again, tactically speaking, better to tell too much in the first draft, tell it all, blab, babble; then in revising consider what merely pads or repeats or slows or impedes your story, and cut it.

It's amazing how long a story a really skilled writer can tell in a few words. Consider Example Seventeen, the life of Mr. Floyd, as told by Virginia Woolf. (Mr. Floyd, the schoolmaster, who is eight years younger than Mrs. Flanders, has proposed to her. Archer, Jacob, and John are her sons; she is a widow.)

EXAMPLE

17

Virginia Woolf: from *Jacob's Room*

"How could I think of marriage!" she said to herself
bitterly, as she fastened the gate with a piece of wire.
She had always disliked red hair in men, she thought,
thinking of Mr. Floyd's appearance, that night when
the boys had gone to bed. And pushing her work-box
away, she drew the blotting-paper towards her, and
read Mr. Floyd's letter again, and her breast went up
and down when she came to the word "love," but not
so fast this time, for she saw Johnny chasing the
geese, and knew that it was impossible for her to
marry any one — let alone Mr. Floyd, who was so
much younger than she was, but what a nice man —
and such a scholar too.

"Dear Mr. Floyd," she wrote. — "Did I forget about
the cheese?" she wondered, laying down her pen. No,
she had told Rebecca that the cheese was in the hall.
"I am much surprised..." she wrote.

But the letter which Mr. Floyd found on the table
when he got up early next morning did not begin "I
am much surprised," and it was such a motherly,
respectful, inconsequent, regretful letter that he kept it
for many years; long after his marriage with Miss
Wimbush, of Andover; long after he had left the
village. For he asked for a parish in Sheffield, which
was given him; and, sending for Archer, Jacob, and
John to say good-bye, he told them to choose whatever they liked in his study to remember him by.
Archer chose a paper-knife, because he did not like to
choose anything too good; Jacob chose the works of
Byron in one volume; John, who was still too young to
make a proper choice, chose Mr. Floyd's kitten, which
his brothers thought an absurd choice, but Mr. Floyd
upheld him when he said: "It has fur like you." Then
Mr. Floyd spoke about the King's Navy (to which

Archer was going); and about Rugby (to which Jacob was going); and next day he received a silver salver and went — first to Sheffield, where he met Miss Wimbush, who was on a visit to her uncle, then to Hackney — then to Maresfield House, of which he became the principal, and finally, becoming editor of a well-known series of Ecclesiastical Biographies, he retired to Hampstead with his wife and daughter, and is often to be seen feeding the ducks on Leg of Mutton Pond. As for Mrs. Flanders's letter — when he looked for it the other day he could not find it, and did not like to ask his wife whether she had put it away. Meeting Jacob in Piccadilly lately, he recognized him after three seconds. But Jacob had grown such a fine young man that Mr. Floyd did not like to stop him in the street.

"Dear me," said Mrs. Flanders, when she read in the *Scarborough and Harrogate Courier* that the Rev. Andrew Floyd, etc., etc., had been made Principal of Maresfield House, "that must be our Mr. Floyd."

A slight gloom fell upon the table. Jacob was helping himself to jam; the postman was talking to Rebecca in the kitchen; there was a bee humming at the yellow flower which nodded at the open window. They were all alive, that is to say, while poor Mr. Floyd was becoming Principal of Maresfield House.

Mrs. Flanders got up and went over to the fender and stroked Topaz on the neck behind the ears.

"Poor Topaz," she said (for Mr. Floyd's kitten was now a very old cat, a little mangy behind the ears, and one of these days would have to be killed).

"Poor old Topaz," said Mrs. Flanders, as he stretched himself out in the sun, and she smiled, thinking how she had had him gelded, and how she did not like red hair in men. Smiling, she went into the kitchen.

Jacob drew rather a dirty pocket-handkerchief across his face. He went upstairs to his room.

Now, the most astonishing and significant thing about this light-speed, single-paragraph biography is that it isn't really about Mr. Floyd at all. It's only there because it casts light on Jacob, the titular subject of the novel — on Jacob's world — and on Jacob's mother, whose voice begins and ends the book. The passage seems playful, and it is. It seems a wandering-off, an irrelevance. A great deal of *Jacob's Room* does. None of it is. Woolf omits the explanations and lets the connections make themselves. She affords an extreme and admirable example of both crowding and leaping. The novel leaps over years at a time, omitting great wads of the protagonist's life. He is seldom the viewpoint character, but we get dropped into the lively minds of many people whose connection with him is left implicit. There is no plot, and the structure is a series of seemingly random glimpses and vignettes. And yet the book moves from the first word to the stunning conclusion as surely and steadily as any Greek tragedy. Whatever she's talking about, Woolf's focus is always Jacob; she never strays from the center; everything in the book contributes to the story she has to tell.

Practice in this kind of "paradoxical focus" was part of the aim of Exercise Nine, Parts Three and Four, "Implication" and the two Lumps.

A Discussion of Story

I define story as a narrative of events (external or psychological) which moves through time or implies the passage of time, and which involves change.

I define plot as a form of story which uses action as its mode, usually in the form of conflict, and which closely and intricately connects one act to another, usually through a causal chain, ending in a climax.

Climax is one kind of pleasure; plot is one kind of story. A strong, shapely plot is a pleasure in itself. It can be reused generation after generation. It provides an armature for narrative that beginning writers may find invaluable.

But most serious modern fictions can't be reduced to a plot, or retold without fatal loss except in their own words. The story is not in the plot but in the telling. It is the telling that moves.

Modernist manuals of writing often conflate story with conflict. This reductionism reflects a culture that inflates aggression and competition while cultivating ignorance of other behavioral options. No narrative of any complexity can be built on or reduced to a single element. Conflict is one kind of behavior. There are others, equally important in any human life, such as relating, finding, losing, bearing, discovering, parting, changing.

Change is the universal aspect of all these sources of story. Story is something moving, something happening, something or somebody changing.

We don't have to have the rigid structure of a plot to tell a story, but we do need *a focus*. What is it about? Who is it about? This focus, explicit or implicit, is the center to which all the events, characters, sayings, doings of the story originally or finally refer. It may be or may not be a simple or a single thing or person or idea. We may not be able to define it. If it's a complex subject it probably can't be expressed in any words at all except all the words of the story. But it is there.

And a story equally needs what Jill Paton Walsh calls *a trajectory* — not necessarily an outline or synopsis to follow, but a movement to follow: the shape of a movement, whether it be straight ahead or roundabout or recurrent or eccentric, a movement which never ceases, from which no passage departs entirely or for long, and to which all passages contribute in some way. This trajectory is the shape of the story as a whole. It moves always to its end, and its end is implied in its beginning.

Crowding and leaping have to do with the focus and the trajectory. Everything that is crowded in to enrich the story sensually, intellectually, emotionally, should be *in focus* — part of the central focus of the story. And every leap should be *along the trajectory*, following the shape and movement of the whole.

I couldn't come up with an exercise specifically aimed at such large considerations about storytelling. But there's one last exercise that's good for us all, though we may not like it much. I shall call it:

A TERRIBLE THING TO DO

Take one of the longer narrative exercises you wrote, perhaps Exercise Seven, Part Four — any one that went over 400 words — and *cut it by half.*

If none of the exercises is suitable, take any piece of narrative prose you have ever written, 400–1000 words, and do this terrible thing to it.

This doesn't mean cutting a little bit here and there, snipping and pruning — though that's part of it. It means counting the words and reducing them to *half that many,* while keeping the narrative clear and the sensory impact vivid, not replacing specifics by generalities, and never using the word "somehow."

If there's dialogue in your piece, cut any long speech or long conversation in half just as implacably.

This kind of cutting is something most professional writers have to do at one time or another. Just for that reason it's good practice. But it's also a real act of self-discipline. It's enlightening. Forced to weigh your words, you find out which are the styrofoam and which are the heavy gold. Severe cutting intensifies your style, forcing you both to crowd and to leap.

Unless you are unusually sparing with your words, or wise and experienced enough to cut as you write, revision will almost always involve some cutting of repetitions, unnecessary explanations, and so on. Consider using revision consciously as a time to consider what *could* go out if it *had* to.

This inevitably includes some of your favorite, most beautiful and admirable sentences and passages. You are allowed to cry or moan softly while you cut them.

Anton Chekhov gave some advice about revising a story: first, he said, throw out the first three pages. As a young writer I figured that if anybody knew about short stories, it was Chekhov, so I tried taking his advice. I really hoped he was wrong, but of course he was right. It depends on the length of the story, naturally; if it's very short, you can only throw out the first three paragraphs. But there are few first drafts to which Chekhov's Razor doesn't apply. Starting a story, we all tend to circle around, explain a lot of stuff, set things up that don't need to be set up. Then we find our way and get going, and *the story begins*...very often just about on page 3.

In revision, as a rough rule, if the beginning can be cut, cut it. And if any passage sticks out in some way, leaves the main trajectory, could possibly come out — take it out and see what the story looks like that way. Often a cut that seemed sure to leave a terrible hole joins up without a seam. It's as if the story, the work itself, has a shape it's trying to achieve, and will take that shape if you'll only clear away the verbiage.

Waving Good-bye from the Pier

Some people see art as a matter of control. I see it mostly as a matter of self-control. It's like this: in me there's a story that wants to be told. It is my end; I am its means. If I can keep myself, my ego, my opinions, my mental junk, out of the way, and find the focus of the story, and follow the movement of the story, the story tells itself.

Everything I've talked about in this book has to do with being ready to let a story tell itself: having the skills, knowing the craft, so that when the magic boat comes by, you can step into it and guide it where it wants to go, where it ought to go.

APPENDIX I:
THE PEER GROUP WORKSHOP

The Members

The optimum number of members for a peer group workshop is probably six or seven up to ten or eleven, meeting once a month or once a fortnight. In a smaller group there are too few different opinions and too many meetings with only two or three attending; with a big group there may be too much to read and the sessions become very long.

In general, a peer group works best if everybody in it is on pretty much the same level of accomplishment. A good deal of variation can be tolerated, even valuable. But members working seriously at their craft will grow discouraged trying to work with people who are just playing at it with no real commitment. Experienced writers may feel bored and exploited having to critique beginner's work, while beginners may be daunted, and wrongly dismissed, by more experienced writers. Big differences in basic familiarity with written style — including punctuation, sentence structure, even spelling — can make such disparities awfully uncomfortable. Yet there are groups that contain wide disparities with no discomfort at all. The great thing is to find the right bunch of people.

Manuscripts

If it's possible to circulate MSS before the workshop meets, do so, giving as long a reading period as possible. This will produce the most thoughtful, useful criticism (much of it written on the MS).

If it's not possible to distribute copies beforehand, the author should bring enough for everybody. Use the first hour of the workshop for a quick read-through of the MSS In a prose workshop, this is definitely preferable to hearing the author read the piece.

Many who work in peer groups will disagree with this last statement. Poets feel it important to hear the piece in the author's voice (I agree), and many prose writers do too. If everybody in your group feels that way, and if reading aloud bonds the group, by all means read at least a few pages of each MS aloud before critique.

But I feel that, though it may be enjoyable to hear how the author's voice "explains" the piece, it's also a waste of the short time of a workshop meeting. The reading is a performance, which may conceal flaws and unclarities. It goes by too fast for most hearers to make useful notes for critiquing. And the fact is, a prose narrative isn't going to be read aloud. It has to explain itself on the page, speak for itself, make itself "heard" by the editor who decides to publish or not publish it, and by all its readers once it's published. (Then, if it's a big success, it might get an audio edition.) If it was written seriously, then it deserves to be read and considered seriously, in solitude, in silence. I consider that kind of slow, silent, thoughtful reading the greatest honor the group can do the piece.

If you have a copy of the MS, write nitpicks, spelling and grammar corrections, and small queries on it. (Remember to sign your name as reader!) First impressions, reactions from a first reading, misunderstandings, can be valuable to the author; don't feel stupid about scribbling them down. Stars or comments of praise for a good phrase or passage can take the sting out of criticisms, which tend to focus on what's wrong. After all, it's just as useful, maybe more useful, to point out what's right.

Make notes for yourself for the critiquing session. Focus on a larger issue or issues, not the nitpicks.

If you're writing exercises in class, this first hour is when you do them; then they're read aloud and critiqued in turn.

Listening

In-class work and short exercises must be read aloud by the author. Listening to a piece in order to criticize it is hard work — very intense, very demanding. Unless scribbling distracts you too much from listening, make notes as you listen for your comments afterwards.

Critiquing

Each critique should be:

Brief.

Strictly in turn.

Without interruption from anyone else.

Centered on some important aspect of the piece. (Write nitpicks on the MS if you have one; if not, keep nitpicking short and sweet.)

Impersonal. (Your knowledge of the author's character or intentions is irrelevant. It's the writing that's under discussion, not the writer. Even if the piece is autobiographical, say "the narrator," not "you.")

Speak to the author, not other people, as you discuss the story.

To be useful, criticism need not be positive, but should lead to the possibility of revision. Sweeping negative judgments on the whole nature or character of the piece are seldom of any use to the author.

(*Private aside:* Certain "writing teachers" go around the country doing Master Classes that consist of the Master reading the students' work and trashing it. The idea is, the Master knows what Art is, and the student is a stupid jerk who can only become an artist if abused by a Master. This sadomasochistic teaching technique exists also in some prestigious writing programs. It has no place in a workshop or peer group. As far as I am concerned it has nothing to do with writing at all, but is a cult of ego-exaltation and ego-abasement.)

Never ask the author a question that might bring forth a long explanation or defense. You may ask the author only a direct, factual, yes-or-no question. You may ask it only if you tell the group your question first and get their consent to ask it. (The reason for this is that others in the group may not want the question answered. Let's say you want to ask, "Did you mean for us not to know who Della's mother is?" Others may prefer to read the text as if they didn't know the author and couldn't ask questions — as we read most narratives — and judge it from that basis.) If you have questions, write them on the MS After all, if the text itself doesn't answer the question, the most useful thing you can do is call attention to the problem, which the author can then fix when revising.

Do tell the writer where you were confused or surprised or annoyed or delighted, which parts you like, what worked for you and what didn't.

Suggestions for how to fix something may be valuable, but should be offered respectfully. Even if you're sure you see just how it ought to be changed, this story belongs to its author, not to you.

Don't say what the story reminds you of in literature or the movies. Respect the text as itself. Consider what this story is about; what it tries to do; how it fulfils itself; how it might achieve its ends better.

Enlarge the group discussion without repeating. If somebody has said what you wanted to say, do say, "I agree with So&so about such&such." If you disagree with a previous speaker, do say so, and explain why.

If you have some members whose critiques are habitually long-winded, you may have to get a kitchen timer and limit each critique to a few minutes. A group that tolerates egocentric, tiresome, blabby critiquing probably won't stay together long. Intensity is essential; interplay is essential.

When people keep their critiques short, the session can end with a general, free discussion. This is often the best part. The discussion may arrive at a "sense of the meeting." But it may end in a dozen different opinions and be just as useful and exciting.

Before and during the entire session, the author of the story under discussion is SILENT.

Offer no preliminary explanations or excuses.

If asked to answer a question, be sure the whole group is willing for you to do so, and be as brief as is humanly possible.

While being critiqued, do make notes of what people say about your story, even if it seems stupid. It may make sense later. Note any comment that keeps coming up from different people.

When all the discussion of your piece is over, you may speak if you want to. Keep it brief. Don't go into defense mode. If you have a question about your story that wasn't addressed, ask it now. In general, the best response to your hardworking critics is "Thank you."

The rule of silence seems arbitrary. It isn't. It is an essential element of the process.

It's almost impossible for an author whose work is being criticised not to be on the defensive, eager to explain, answer, point out — "Oh, but see, what I meant was...." "Oh, I was going to do that in the next draft...." If you can't do this you won't waste time (yours and theirs) trying to do it. Instead, you will listen. You won't be busy mentally preparing what you're going to say in answer, because you can't answer. All you can do is hear. You can hear what people got from your piece, what they think needs some work, what they misunderstood and understood, disliked and liked about it. And that's what you're there for.

If you truly can't endure the rule of silence, probably you don't really want to know how other people respond to your work. You choose to be the first and last judge of it. In this case, you won't fit happily in a group. This is absolutely OK. It's a matter of temperament. Some artists can work only in solitude. Also, there may be periods in an artist's life when they need the stimulus and feedback of a group, and periods when they do better working alone. Always, in the last analysis, you are your own judge, and you make your own decisions. The practice of art is true freedom.

Start with a volunteer author's piece, and go right round from there to every person who submitted a piece.

The critiquing also goes clear round the circle, every person speaking about every piece. Reverse directions from time to time. (With a large group in a limited time, it may be necessary to use devices such as having only every second person speak.)

Ideally, free critique is possible — only those speaking who want to, with no time limit on the critique and no order of rotation. But don't try it until you all know that nobody in the group is habitually silent or eternally blabby and that nobody is allowed to bully. Mutual respect and trust is absolutely essential to a workshop, and free critique does permit egos to overexpand. Many peer groups do regular mutual critiquing for years using the right-round-the-circle mode as the fairest and least stressful.

All the successful groups I know also are strict about keeping each critique brief, and implacable about silencing the author. Adhesive tape is usually not necessary.

APPENDIX II:
FORMS OF THE VERB

FOR A CLEAR, THOROUGH EXPLANATION, WITH EXAMPLES, OF ENGLISH VERB forms, see *Harper's English Grammar*, by John B. Opdycke. Many of the books calling themselves "Grammars" are actually manuals of style and usage, and give sketchy, patchy information about basic matters such as verb tenses. Opdycke's book is the best real reference on English grammar I have found. Unfortunately, you'll have to go to a library or a used bookstore or electronic bookfinder service to find it.

Because I suspect that some people are daunted by the mere names of the tenses, I provide the simple conjugation (omitting some hardly-ever-used forms) of a regular verb. We recognize the meaning and use of all these forms, though we may not know their formal names. I hope it may be interesting and even reassuring to see them all set out this way. If it's merely bewildering, focus on one of the tenses at a time. I'll bet you know how to use it and have no trouble making a sentence to go around it. You might try doing so.

I use the regular verb *change* as the example. Regular verbs in English are nice: Except for a couple of tenses where the third person singular is different, all the persons are the same in each tense. (The verb *be,* used in progressive tenses and the passive voice, has several irregular forms, but if you speak English, you know them all.)

Active Voice • Infinitives
PRESENT INFINITIVE: to change
PAST INFINITIVE: to have changed

Active Voice • Participles
PRESENT PARTICIPLE: changing
PAST PARTICIPLE: changed
PERFECT PARTICIPLE: having changed

Active Voice • Indicative Mood
PRESENT TENSE: I, you, we, they change (he, she, it changes)
PAST TENSE: I, you, he/she/it, we, they changed
FUTURE TENSE: I, you, he/she/it, we, they will change
PRESENT PERFECT TENSE: I, you, we, they have changed; he/she/it has changed
PAST PERFECT TENSE: I, you, he/she/it, we, they had changed
FUTURE PERFECT TENSE: I, you, he/she/it, we, they will have changed

Active Voice • Subjunctive Mood (with *if, that, lest, though, till, unless, should,* and in certain constructions)
PRESENT TENSE: If I, you, he/she/it, we, they change
PAST TENSE: *same as the indicative*
FUTURE TENSE: If I, you, he/she/it, we, they should change
PRESENT PERFECT TENSE: If I, you, he/she/it, we they have changed
PAST PERFECT TENSE: *same as the indicative*
FUTURE PERFECT TENSE: If I, you, he/she/it, we, they should have changed

Active Voice • Potential Mood (alone or with *hope, fear, be possible that,* etc.)
PRESENT TENSE: I, you, he/she/it, we, they may change, can change
PAST TENSE: I, you, he/she/it, we, they might change, could change
PRESENT PERFECT TENSE: I, you, he/she/it,we, they may have changed
PAST PERFECT TENSE: I, you, he/she/it, we, they might have changed

Active Voice • Imperative Mood
(Second person only) change!

Passive Voice • Infinitives
PRESENT INFINITIVE: to be changed
PAST INFINITIVE: to have been changed

Passive Voice • Participles
PRESENT PARTICIPLE: being changed
PAST PARTICIPLE: being changed
PAST PERFECT PARTICIPLE: having been changed

Passive Voice • Indicative Mood
PRESENT TENSE: I am, you are, he/she/it is, we, you, they are changed
PAST TENSE: I was, you were, he/she/it was, we, you, they were changed
FUTURE TENSE: I, you, he/she/it, we, they will be changed
PRESENT PERFECT TENSE: I, you, we, they have; he/she/it has been changed
PAST PERFECT TENSE: I, you, he/she/it, we, they had been changed
FUTURE PERFECT TENSE: I, you, he/she/it, we, they will have been changed

Passive Voice • Subjunctive Mood
PRESENT TENSE: if I, you, he/she/it, we, they be changed
PAST TENSE: if I, you, he/she/it, we, they were changed
FUTURE TENSE: if I, you, he/she/it, we, they should be changed
PRESENT PERFECT TENSE: if I, you, he/she/it, we, they have been changed
PAST PERFECT TENSE: if I, you, he/she/it, we, they had been changed
FUTURE PERFECT TENSE: if I, you, he/she/it, we, they should have been changed

Passive Voice • Potential Mood
PRESENT TENSE: I, you, he/she/it, we, they may be changed
PAST TENSE: I, you, he/she/it, we, they might be changed
PRESENT PERFECT TENSE: I, you, he/she/it, we, they may have been changed
PAST PERFECT TENSE: I, you, he/she/it, we, they might have been changed

<u>Passive Voice</u> • <u>Imperative Mood</u>
(Second person only) be changed!

❖ ❖ ❖

Here is a synopsis (using first person only) of the progressive conjugation, which is formed by adding the present participle of the verb *change* to every form of the verb *be*.

<u>Active Voice</u> • <u>Indicative Mood</u>
PRESENT TENSE: I am changing
PAST TENSE: I was changing
FUTURE TENSE: I will be changing
PRESENT PERFECT TENSE: I have been changing
PAST PERFECT TENSE: I had been changing
FUTURE PERFECT TENSE: I will have been changing

<u>Active Voice</u> • <u>Subjunctive Mood</u>
PRESENT TENSE: If I be changing
PAST TENSE: If I were changing
FUTURE TENSE: If I should be changing
PRESENT PERFECT TENSE: If I have been changing
PAST PERFECT TENSE: If I had been changing
FUTURE PERFECT TENSE: If I should have been changing

<u>Active Voice</u> • <u>Potential Mood</u>
PRESENT TENSE: I may be changing
PAST TENSE: I might be changing
PRESENT PERFECT TENSE: I may have been changing
PAST PERFECT TENSE: I might have been changing

The progressive conjugation in the passive voice has only a few forms in common use, such as the present: I am being changed, or the past: I was being changed.

❖ ❖ ❖

This list is pretty formidable so long as it is in the abstract. It may come alive for you if you just try using the examples in sentences. For instance:

We have changed 4,302,116 diapers.

By next summer, we will have been changing diapers for five years straight.

Would you prefer to have been changed into a duck?

I warn you that if she should be changed into a swan, she will not mate with a duck.

And so on. Use other verbs, too, if you enjoy this game.

Despite their marvelous complexity, the forms given above are certainly not the only ways to use verbs. There is the "customary past," formed with used to or would — I used to change, I would change. There are the progressive or intentional forms using *go* — I am going to change. There are the emphatic forms using *do* — I do change, I did change. And all the negatives and the interrogatives of the simple tenses are formed with do — I do not change, I did not change; do I change? did I change? And so on and on. Please don't be alarmed by this exuberant complexity. The first time you saw a diagram of all the muscles and nerves involved in lifting your finger, you might wonder how you ever did it; but in fact you do know how to lift your finger. Same with verbs.

Some Notes on Verbs

A Note Concerning the Subjunctive

The indicative generally states that something did or didn't happen; the Subjunctive generally says that something might happen, or wouldn't it be wonderful if it did happen, or it could only happen if something else happened. The Subjunctive covers all kinds of contingent, shadowy states. If you know its uses in one of the Romance languages, for example, you know what subtle, powerful shades of meaning the Subjunctive makes possible. In modern English we mostly use auxiliary verbs to get these effects, perhaps because our Subjunctive in English differs in so few places from the Indicative. "Purists" of language cling to these remnants. If you write "I wish I was dead," editors and pundits may correct you — "You mean, 'I wish I were dead.'" It would be rude to reply that you wish they were dead; but you may fairly state that the Subjunctive in English, if not dead, has a bad case of rigor mortis.

A Note Concerning the Potential Mood

"I think he may come" and "I thought he might come" mean the same thing in two different time-frames: the speaker considers/considered an uncertain future event to be possible.

"I think he might come" is a colloquial usage with the same or nearly the same meaning as "I think he may come."

The present potential, "may," is increasingly often used in a past-tense context: "I thought he may come." To my ear, this is an impossible combination; it self-destructs. I hear "may" as a form having to do with the future of the present, not the future of the past. I can be comfortable with it only if written, "I thought, 'He may come.'" "May" is, however, now so frequently used in a past-tense context that this distinction between "might" and "may" may well be a goner.

A Note Concerning the Verbs Lie and Lay

I belong to the last generation that flinches when it hears "I'm laying down," or "Leave it lay." For younger people who retain a vague uneasiness or curiosity concerning this usage, here's a note about it. There are three verbs, one of which isn't really involved:

1. To *lie*, an intransitive verb (it can't have a direct object), meaning to tell an untruth. I lie, lied, will lie, have lied, am lying. — I lie about my income to the IRS. Last night I lied to you. He was lying about the gun. — This verb is far away enough in meaning from the other two that it doesn't get tangled with them.

But the other two, related in meaning, are by now hopelessly mixed up.

2. To *lie*, an intransitive verb (it can't have a direct object) meaning to be recumbent or prone, or to be on top of something. I lie, lay, will lie, have lain, am lying. — I'm lying down to sleep.

The egg lies in the nest. The book lay on the shelf all night. He was lying around cleaning his gun.

3. To *lay*, a transitive verb (it has to have a direct object), meaning to set or put something down, or put something onto something else. I lay, laid, will lay, have laid, am laying. — Now I lay me down to sleep. The sparrow lays an egg. Last night I laid the book on the shelf. He was laying the gun down when it went off. (The direct objects are: me, egg, book, gun.)

What's happened is that the transitive verb about setting an object down has got tangled into the intransitive verb about being horizontal not vertical, and made a total hash of it, and is now devouring the hash.

If you don't flinch when you read "She just laid there" (or the rare but even more painful overcorrection, "She has lain the gun on the table"), consider yourself lucky. There really is nothing to be done about it by now, I think, except flinch.

A Note on the Combination of Tenses

Getting two different times into a clear relationship — combining two tenses — is what seems to worry people most about verbs. Perhaps Opdycke's definitions will help.

The present perfect tense "indicates an action begun in the past and extending to the time the statement is made."

Example: At one o'clock I realize that she has talked nonstop for an hour. Or, in the present perfect progressive: At one o'clock I realize that she has been talking for an hour.

The past perfect tense "indicates an action completed earlier than some other past time."

Example: At one o'clock I realized that she had talked nonstop for an hour. Or, in the past perfect progressive: At one o'clock I realized that she had been talking for an hour.

The past perfect — had talked, had gone, had been — seems to be the one that worries people most, and I don't know why. Is it because it often involves saying "had had"? — "He had had a bad time before he met her." Even in quite formal writing, where the writer doesn't say "doesn't" or "it's," I often see this elided to "He'd had," as if there were something evil or unnatural about the past perfect of *have*. There isn't. It's no more uncomfortable to the ear than any other unelided verb. I don't know what the problem is.

The future perfect tense "indicates an action to be completed at some definite time in the future." Example: She will have seen the report before she decides. This usage is exact and formal. In colloquial speech and writing the simple future will do — She will see the report before she decides.

Most of the awkwardness of using the present tense in narration has to do with these statements that involve two different times. The close focus of the present tense makes it hard to include any time but the present. "At one o'clock I realize that she has talked for an hour" — fine. But if she started at noon and stopped at one and I don't think about it until six, I can only say, "At six I realize that she had talked for an hour," which combines a present with a past perfect, something that happens only in writing, and therefore sounds and is stilted or literary. In past tense narration there's no problem; whether I realized it at one o'clock, or six o'clock, or next week, it's "I realized that she had talked for an hour." (This is an example of why I use the terms focussed and inclusive for these tenses in narration.)

❖ ❖ ❖

At the beginning of one of my books I wrote, "The people in this book might be going to have lived a long, long time from now in Northern California." If I've got it right, that's the active voice, progressive conjugation, potential mood, present tense, third person plural of go inflecting the past infinitive of *live*.

I deliberately used this magnificent conglomeration of verbiage to establish myself and the reader as being in the complex situation of pretending to look back in time on some fictional people whom we pretend might exist in a time very far in our future. You can say all that with a couple of verb forms. (The Northern California part is extra.)

The copy editor was amazingly civil about my grand verb. One reviewer apparently was unable to get to the end of it, and whined about it. Others cited it with what I hope was amusement or admiration. I still like it. It was the shortest way to say exactly what I meant. That's what verbs, in all their moods and tenses, are for.

GLOSSARY

Affect

A noun, with the accent on the first syllable, it means feeling, emotion. It doesn't mean effect.

Alliteration

"Peter Piper picked a peck of pickled peppers" is an alliterative sentence. So is "Great big gobs of greasy grimy gopher guts."

Armature

A frame, like the steel frame of a skyscraper.

Articulated

Connected, joined together, as in "an articulated skeleton" and "an articulated bus."

Clause

A clause is a group of words that has a subject and a predicate.

The first part of that sentence — "A clause is a group of words" — can stand alone and so is called the main clause. Its subject is the noun "A clause." Its predicate is the verb "is." Because it's the main clause, those are also considered to be the subject and predicate of the sentence as a whole.

A subordinate clause can't stand alone but relates to the main clause. In the sentence above, the subordinate clause is "that has a subject and a predicate." Its subject is "that" and its predicate is "has."

Clauses can relate to one another in complicated ways when expressing complicated thoughts or situations, and those which turn up inside one another, like Chinese boxes, which you open only to find yet another box inside, are said to be "embedded."

(The embedded clause in that sentence is "which you open only to find yet another box inside.")

Colloquial

Spoken language as contrasted to written language; or, in writing, an easygoing, informal tone that imitates speech. The two Mark Twain pieces in our examples are beautiful pieces of colloquial writing. Most narrative, even if not highly formal, is not fully colloquial.

Critiquing

The process of discussing a piece of writing in a Workshop or Peer group. (See Appendix I.) This peculiar word replaced "criticising," maybe because "criticise" and "criticism" have gathered a negative charge, while "critique" and "critiquing" still sound neutral.

Dingbat

We all know some dingbats. But dingbats are also decorative elements in type, little figures or devices that typesetters use for various reasons, often to stick in between paragraphs or sections to make a break look nice. Like this:

❖ ❖ ❖

Embedded Clause

See Clauses.

Grammar

The fundamental system of a language; the rules for using words so that they make sense. People can have good grammatical sense without knowing the rules, but to break the rules wisely, you have to know the rules well. Knowledge is freedom.

Metaphor

An implied comparison or description. Instead of saying A is like B, you say A is B, or you use B to refer to A. So, instead of "She's as mild and docile and lovable as a lamb," you say, "She's a lamb." Instead of "I'm reading bits here and there like a cow eating bits of grass here and there," you say, "I'm browsing through the book."

A great deal of language usage is metaphorical. Most insults are metaphors: "You dingbat!" "That old fart." One thing writers have to watch for is the common, "dead" metaphors which when mixed come dreadfully alive: "Everybody in this department is going to have to put on his thinking cap, get down to brass tacks, and kick ass."

Meter

A regular rhythm or beat. Lub-dub - lub-dub.... ta DUM ta DUM ta DUM.... tiddy-dum, tiddy-dum, tiddy DUM DUM DUM.... If prose develops meter for more than a few words in a row, it stops being prose and turns into poetry, whether you want it to or not.

Le Mot Juste

French for "the right word."

Onomatopoeia

A word that sounds like what it means, like "sizzle" or "hiss" or "slurp," is onomatopoeic. As for the word onomatopoeia, it sounds like onna-matta-peeya.

Parts of Speech

Classes of words, determined by their use in the sentence, such as noun, pronoun, verb, adverb, adjective, preposition. Such words may bring back horrid memories of school, but it's impossible to criticise grammar or understand criticism of grammar without this vocabulary.

Pathetic Fallacy

A phrase, too often used condescendingly, to describe a passage of writing in which the landscape, weather, etc., mirror or embody human emotions.

Peer Group

A group of writers who meet regularly to read and discuss one another's writing, forming a leaderless Workshop. (See Appendix I.)

Person (of the Verb)

The English verb has six persons, three in the singular number and three in the plural. Here are examples of a regular verb (work) and an irregular verb (be) in the present and past tenses.

first singular: I work; I am / I worked; I was
second singular: you work; you are / you worked; you were
third singular: he, she, it works; he, she, it is / he, she, it worked; he, she, it was
first plural: we work; we are / we worked; we were
second plural: you work; you are / you worked; you were
third plural: they work; they are / they worked; they were

Person and number affect the verb forms only in the third person singular of the present tense, and the singular of the irregular verb to be.

Sentence Fragment

A piece of sentence used in place of a whole sentence.

A sentence has a subject (a noun or pronoun or person's name) and a predicate (a verb). (The subject of that sentence is "sentence" and the predicate is "has.") A fragment lacks either the subject or the predicate or both:

No sentence fragments!

Going where?

Too late, too late.

We use them all the time in talking, and in writing too; but in writing, what's left out must be clearly implied by the context around the fragment. Repeated use of fragments in narrative tends to sound either awkward or affected.

Simile

A comparison using "like" or "as": "She turned as red as a turkey." "My love is like a red, red rose." The difference between simile and metaphor is that the comparison or description is open in simile — "I watch like a hawk" — while in metaphor the "like" or "as" disappears: "I am a camera."

Stream of Consciousness

A name for a fictional mode or voice developed by the novelists Dorothy Richardson and James Joyce, in which the reader participates in the moment-to-moment experience, reactions, and thoughts of the viewpoint character. Though very constrictive when used throughout a whole novel, passages of stream of consciousness are common and effective in long works, and the mode is well suited to short pieces and present-tense narration.

Syntax

"(2.) The arrangement of words (in their appropriate forms) by which their connexion and relation in a sentence are shown." —*The Shorter Oxford English Dictionary*.

Recognition of syntactical constructions used to be taught by the method of diagramming, a useful skill for any writer. If you can find an old grammar book that shows you how to diagram a sentence, have a look; it's enlightening. It may make you realize that a sentence has a skeleton, just as a horse does; and the sentence, or the horse, moves the way it does because of the way its bones are put together.

A keen feeling for that arrangement and connection and relation of words is essential equipment for a writer of narrative prose. You don't need to know all the rules of syntax, but you have to train yourself to hear it or feel it — so that you'll know when a sentence is so tangled up it's about to fall onto its nose, and when it's running clear and free.

Tenses

The forms of a verb that indicate the times at which the action is supposed to be happening. See Appendix II.

ABOUT THE AUTHOR: URSULA K. LE GUIN

URSULA KROEBER WAS BORN IN 1929 IN BERKELEY, CALIFORNIA, WHERE she grew up. Her parents were the anthropologist Alfred Kroeber and the author Theodora Kroeber, author of *Ishi*. She went to Radcliffe College and did graduate work at Columbia University. She married Charles A. Le Guin, a historian, in Paris in 1953; they have lived in Portland, Oregon, since 1958, and have three children and three grandchildren.

Ursula K. Le Guin has written poetry and fiction all her life. Her first publications were poems, and in the 1960s she began to publish short stories and novels. She writes both poetry and prose, and in various modes, including realistic fiction, science fiction, fantasy, young children's books, books for young adults, screenplays, essays, verbal texts for musicians, and voicetexts for performance or recording. As of 1997 she has published over a hundred short stories (collected in eight volumes), two collections of essays, ten books for children, five volumes of poetry, and sixteen novels. Among the honors her writing has received are a National Book Award, five Hugo and five Nebula Awards, the Kafka Award, a Pushcart Prize, and the Howard Vursell Award of the American Academy of Arts and Letters.

Her occupations, she says, are writing, reading, housework, and teaching. She is a feminist, a conservationist, and a Western American, passionately involved with West Coast literature, landscape, and life.

EIGHTH MOUNTAIN books can be found in independent and chain bookstores across the United States, Canada, Great Britain, and Australia. If your favorite bookstore is out of the title you want, ask them to order it for you. You can also order books directly from Eighth Mountain if you are anywhere in North America. Please add $2.50 for the first book ($3.50 in Canada) and 50¢ each additional book for postage and handling. Send a check payable to the Eighth Mountain Press. Books will be mailed U.S. Postal "special fourth class" (or "printed matter surface" to Canada). If you need speedier delivery, call us to discuss other options.

Eighth Mountain titles are distributed to the trade by Consortium Book Sales and Distribution, 1045 Westgate Drive, Saint Paul, MN 55114-1065 (800/283-3572 or 612/221-9035) and are carried by all major book wholesalers and library jobbers.

For specialty, bulk, and catalog sales contact the Eighth Mountain Press directly.

The Eighth Mountain Press
624 SE 29th Avenue
Portland, OR 97214
phone: 503/233-3936
fax: 503/233-0774